JUDGE
JUDGE DREDD
SLEEPING
(A GRIM FAIRY T
ONCE UPON A TIME, THERE WAS A DASHING YOUNG PRINCE CALLED VINCE.
MUTY CUNTRI
MEGA CITY 1
NOW PRINCE VINCE WAS SO HANDSOME THAT HIS BEAUTY COULD NOT BE CONTAINED IN ONLY ONE FACE. SO OLD MOTHER NATURE, IN HER KINDNESS, HAD GIVEN HIM TWO.
ME
NO ENTR
ONE DAY, OUT ON A QUEST ON HIS FAITHFUL STEED DAVE, PRINCE VINCE CAME TO A GRIM AND FOREBODING CITY WHERE THE SINISTER INHABITANTS GREETED HIM WITH SCORN--
WHERE YOU THINK YOU'RE GOIN', FREAK ? THIS CITY'S OFF-LIMITS TO MUTANTS !
BEAT IT !
I AM PRINCE VINCE, HEIR TO THE WESTLANDS, ENGAGED ON A DANGEROUS QUEST.
I HAVE SWORN NEVER TO RETURN HOME UNTIL I HAVE FOUND MY SWEET-HEART, THE LOST LADY PENELOPE !
SHE CAME THIS WAY A YEAR SINCE. KNOW YOU OF HER ?

CREEP MUST BE FROM ONE OF THE TRIBES LIVIN' OUT IN THE CURSED EARTH. RADIATION MUST'VE DRIVEN HIM CRAZY!
PENELOPE..? LAST YEAR..?
YOUR GIRLFRIEND GOT BLONDE HAIR, BLUE EYES AN' GREEN SKIN?
INDEED! KNOW YOU WHERE SHE IS?
SURE. IN A JUSTICE DEPT CRYO-CUBE!
IMPRISONED? BUT THERE MUST BE SOME MISTAKE--
NO MISTAKE, MUTIE!
STAND WHERE YOU ARE! YOU'RE UNDER ARREST!
BUT PRINCE VINCE HAD NOT JOURNEYED SO FAR, AND FACED SO MANY PERILS, JUST TO END UP IN A MEGA-CITY CELL--
WE'RE GOING IN, DAVE! SWITCH TO AERIAL MODE!
GRUD ON A GREENIE!
HE'S GOING OVER THE WALL! BRING HIM DOWN!

I HAD HOPED TO AVOID BLOODSHED, VILE ONES! BUT YOU HAVE BROUGHT IT UPON YOUR OWN HEADS--
SO SAYING, VINCE SMOTE THEM WITH THE MAGIC SWORD HE'D FOUND IN THE RUINS OF THE MYSTERIOUS TEMPLE OF THE MISSILE SILO--
FRZZZ!
BAWUUUM!
AAAH!
AAAGH!
TAKE COVER!
FRZZZ!
DREDD TO CONTROL! WE GOT A MUTIE ON A WINGED HORSE JUST CROSSED THE WEST WALL! ALERT H-WAGONS—HE'S ARMED WITH A MILITARY PHASE-LASER!
PROBABLE DESTINATION—THE CRYO CUBES! TAKE HIM ALIVE IF POSSIBLE!
OVER THE CITY WALL, PRINCE VINCE GASPED IN AWE. NEVER IN HIS LIFE HAD HE SEEN SUCH MIGHTY BUILDINGS, SUCH WONDEROUS SIGHTS!
HO, CITIZEN! I AM A STRANGER IN THIS CITY! WHERE WILL I FIND THE EVIL TOWER OF ULTIMATE COLD?
THE CRYO-CUBES? SHEESH, BUDDY—THE JUDGES MIGHT NOT TAKE IT TOO KINDLY IF I SAY!

TELL YOU WHAT, THOUGH — 'S MAKE A DEAL. MY BATWINGS AND THE INFO YOU WANT, IN RETURN FOR THE FLYIN' HORSE!
THOUGH IT NEAR BROKE HIS HEART, PRINCE VINCE CONSENTED TO THE SWAP. FOR THOUGH HE AND DAVE HAD BEEN TOGETHER MANY YEARS, WHEN ALL WAS SAID AND DONE DAVE WAS JUST A FLYING HORSE--
WHILE PENELOPE WAS THE FAIREST MAID IN ALL THE WORLD.
STRAIGHT ON ABOUT 200 METRES — THAT DARK BUILDING WITH THE **CRYO-VAULTS** SIGN ON THE SIDE!
CRYO
CUBES
THERE HE IS!
READY THE NETS! HIT HIM WITH **STUN**!
SO LONG, SUCKER! **AAAAAAAAGH!**
GOTCHA, CREEP!

H-WAGON TO DREDD! WE GOT PRINCE PERP ON THE FLYIN' STEED!
OH YEAH..?
DREDD
NO IRON BARS SHALL KEEP ME FROM MY LOVE!
LADY PENELOPE'S CELL — WHERE?
P-PENELOPE? TH-THE MUTANT?
SHE'S TWO LEVELS DOWN — K-13!
LEVEL-7
E-K
AT LAST! AFTER THEIR LONG MONTHS APART, HE AND PENELOPE WOULD BE TOGETHER AGAIN. HIS YOUNG HEART POUNDED FIT TO BURST FROM HIS CHEST--
PENELOPE! FAIREST FLOWER OF ALL THE WEST! OH MY LOVE, WHAT HAVE THESE MONSTERS DONE TO YOU? YOU, SO LOVELY, SO INNOCENT--
INNOCENT MY BUTT!

YOUR GIRLFRIEND SNEAKED INTO THE CITY LOOKIN' TO BUY TIMERS FOR A GUIDED MISSILE. SHE TRIED TO FIGHT HER WAY OUT WHEN WE RUMBLED HER SCAM--
TOOK A BULLET IN THE BRAIN BEFORE WE COULD FIND OUT WHERE SHE CAME FROM—AND WHERE THIS MISSILE IS!
SHE'S BEING HELD HERE IN SUSPENDED ANIMATION UNTIL OUR MEDICS CAN MAKE HER WELL ENOUGH FOR INTERROGATION!
BARBARIAN! HOW DARE YOU TREAT A LADY THUS?
GUESS IT DOESN'T MATTER NOW, CREEP--
YOU CAN ANSWER ALL OUR QUESTIONS FOR HER!
AAAAGH!
CONTROL—PREPARE AN INTERROGATION CUBE. YOU GOT A DOUBLE INFORMANT COMING IN!
AN' YOU CAN SWITCH OFF THE FROG IN K-13!
NOT SURPRISINGLY, NONE OF THEM LIVED HAPPY EVER AFTER.
THE END.

NU EARTH. THE MOROKK DESERT. SCENE OF A FRONT LINE IN THE ETERNAL FUTURE WAR BETWEEN NORTS AND SOUTHERS.
KYRO
TIMBUK-2
WALKING THE WASTED LAND IS THE LAST SURVIVING GI (GENETIC INFANTRYMAN), A SOUTHER TROOPER 'GONE ROGUE'.
NOTHING FOR US HERE, GUYS.
HIS HELMET, BACKPACK AND GUN CONTAINED BIO-CHIPS OF HIS THREE, DEAD GI COMRADES.
KYRO CITY AHEAD, ROGUE. ZONAL CAPITAL OF THIS AREA.
WE'LL JUST PASS ON THROUGH, HELM. NO NEED TO GET CAUGHT UP IN ANY TROUBLE.
BUT, IN THE CITY. . .
SOUTHER CONVOYS, MOVING UP TO THE FRONT...
YOU SAID WE WERE PASSING THROUGH, ROGUE...
ROGUE TROOPER
MAYBE I SHOULD OFFER MY SERVICES — LOOKS BIG.
GOOD LUCK BOYS
NAIL ME A NORT
HOLD ON, ROGUE! REMEMBER YOU'RE STILL CLASSIFIED AS A...
DESERTER!
THE GASBAH Part ONE
2000 A.D. Credit Card:
SCRIPT ROBOT GERRY FINLEY-DAY
ART ROBOT CAM KENNEDY
LETTERING ROBOT BILL NUTTALL
COMPU-73E

IT'S THE GI. THERE'S A PRICE ON HIS HEAD!
YOU'RE UNDER ARREST!
MILITARY FUZZ. DAMMIT.
HALT! THIS IS A FRONT LINE CITY— WE CAN SHOOT ON SIGHT!
SOUTHERS
GO! GO! GO!
GOTTA MOVE. I AIN'T GONNA BE SHOT BY MY OWN SIDE.
THICKER CLOUDS AHEAD. I CAN LOSE MYSELF IN THEM.
OF COURSE, THIS IS THE CITY'S 'GASBAH'! THE LOW-LYING AREA THAT COLLECTS THE DIRTIEST CHEM-CLOUD CONCENTRATIONS!
AHEAD...
CHECKPOINT
MF CONTROL
ROGER, CONTROL. DESERTER HEADING THIS WAY. WE'LL STOP HIM.
SORRY TO DISAPPOINT YOU, FUZZBALLS!
WHA-?
HE'S THROUGH! NO POINT GIVING CHASE, WE'D NEVER FIND HIM IN...
...THE GASBAH!

THE CHEM-CLOUDS THIN AND...
GADA?
TUM, TUM!
THIS IS WHERE OFF-WORLDERS ARE CONFINED. I SHOULD BE SAFE NOW.
THE ALIENS ARE DESCENDANTS OF THOSE WHO WERE TRAPPED ON NU EARTH WHEN THE WAR STARTED.
LIKE ME THEY CAN BREATHE THIS CHEM-SOUP, SO THEY DON'T GET BOTHERED BY THE MILITARY FUZZ.
HGFAI-XXX?
BAGMAN, RUN THIS THROUGH YOUR TRANSLATOR COMP.
ROGUE'S BACK-PACK CONTAINED AN ADVANCED TRANSLATIONS COMPUTER, AMONG OTHER THINGS.
HE'S MANGANESE ...ASKING WHAT KIND OF HUMAN YOU ARE. I TOLD HIM.
BETTER LEAVE THIS CONVERSATION TO ME. ⟨XXKKX BRHGGA HU TYYR IO?⟩
GAHSAAA? GAHSAA?
I ASKED HIM WHERE THE NEAREST BAR IS. I FIGURED YOU NEEDED A DRINK AFTER ALL THAT DESERT SAND!
HE SAID IT WAS JUST PAST THE MARKET PLACE-BOY, HIGH CHEM-COUNT HERE!
RIX-BAH
THIS MUST BE IT. JUDGING BY THE NOISE, IT'S A POPULAR PLACE.
HMM, ONLY A COUPLE OF HUMES. BAR-TENDER AND A BUBBLE DANCER IN A SEAL. MUST BE PAID WELL TO WORK IN THE GASBAH.

COUGH HEARD OF YOU, DESERTER. HUMANS AIN'T WELCOME HERE. COUGH I'M A CHEM-VET. COUGH ONLY DREGS LIKE ME LIVE HERE.
'FRIENDLY' PLACE, HUH, ROGUE?
CHEM-VET: SOLDIER DISABLED BY CHEMICAL WARFARE.
HSGAHAA!
DO, DO!
LOOKS LIKE I'M NOT THE ONLY UNWELCOME ONE HERE. THOSE BIG ALIS ARE BULLYING THAT SMALL ONE.
"ALI"—ARMY SLANG FOR ALIENS.
GRAAL! GRAALA!
ONE'S COMING OVER HERE.
HE'S TALKING IN BRUTUL—I'LL TRANSLATE!
<IT'S THE GI WE WERE TOLD OF! HE'S NOT WELCOME HERE!>
<SHOULD WE THROW HIM OUT, OR GIVE HIM TO THE HUMAN MFs?>
<WE MIGHT GET A REWARD!>
HMMM—
BAGMAN—
DAHA FFHAA FHE! <LOOK BEHIND YOU, STUPID!>
THWUDD!
UHHHGGGG!
THANKS, BAGMAN. I NEEDED THAT DIVERSION.

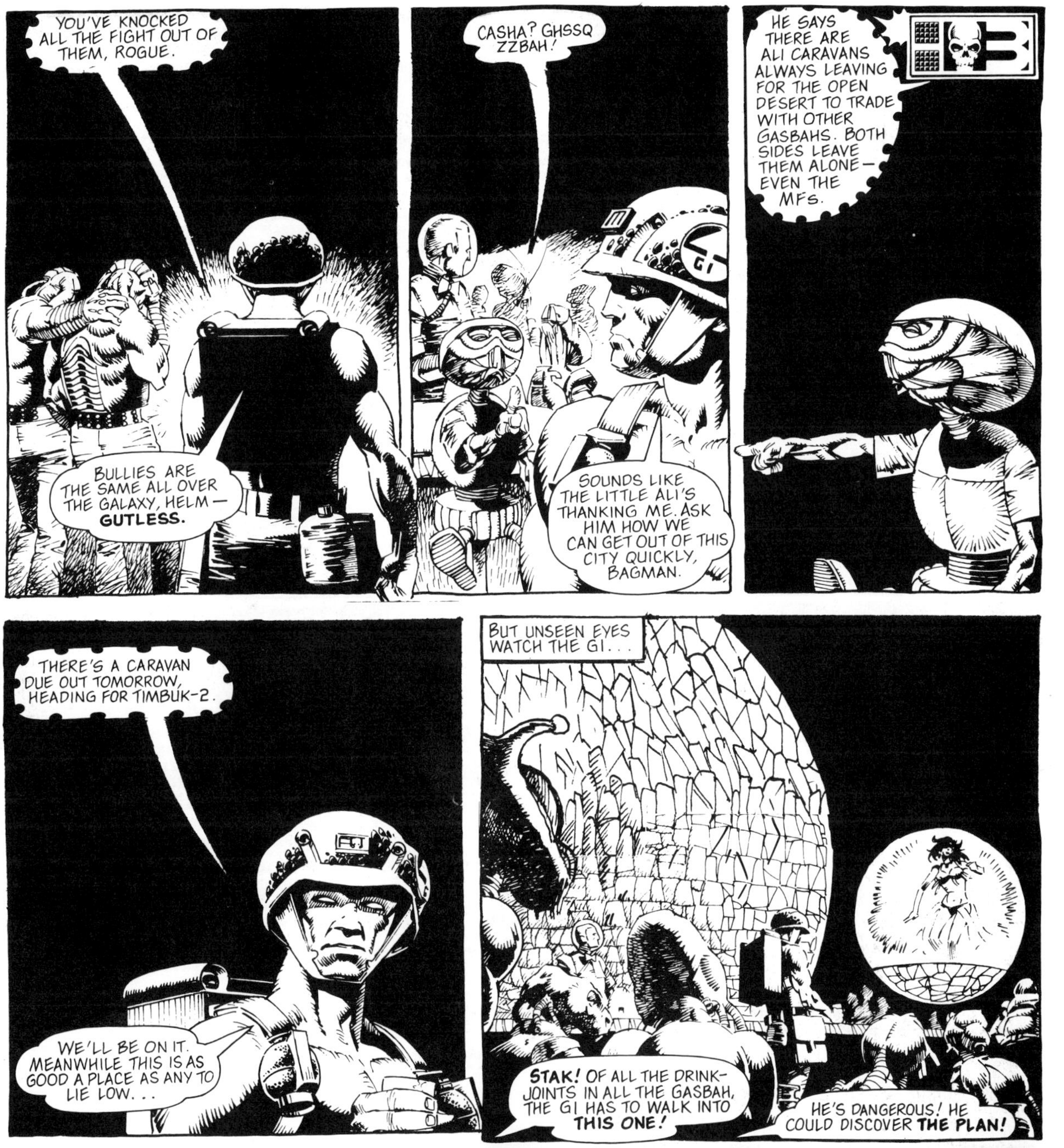
YOU'VE KNOCKED ALL THE FIGHT OUT OF THEM, ROGUE.
BULLIES ARE THE SAME ALL OVER THE GALAXY, HELM— **GUTLESS.**
CASHA? GHSSQ ZZBAH!
SOUNDS LIKE THE LITTLE ALI'S THANKING ME. ASK HIM HOW WE CAN GET OUT OF THIS CITY QUICKLY, BAGMAN.
HE SAYS THERE ARE ALI CARAVANS ALWAYS LEAVING FOR THE OPEN DESERT TO TRADE WITH OTHER GASBAHS. BOTH SIDES LEAVE THEM ALONE— EVEN THE MFs.
THERE'S A CARAVAN DUE OUT TOMORROW, HEADING FOR TIMBUK-2.
WE'LL BE ON IT. MEANWHILE THIS IS AS GOOD A PLACE AS ANY TO LIE LOW...
BUT UNSEEN EYES WATCH THE GI...
STAK! OF ALL THE DRINK-JOINTS IN ALL THE GASBAH, THE GI HAS TO WALK INTO **THIS ONE!**
HE'S DANGEROUS! HE COULD DISCOVER **THE PLAN!**
NOT IF WE'RE **CLEVER**. THIS PLACE IS TEEMING WITH ALIEN LIFE. HUMANS AREN'T LIKED—MIGHT EVEN GET **KILLED— ESPECIALLY A GI!**

DROIDS LIFESTYLE QUESTIONNAIRE

DESIGNATION *Kevin Hopgood*

FAVOURITE 2000 AD STORY

Dead Man

FAVOURITE FOODS

1. *Pizza*
2. *Pizza*
3. *More Pizza*

FAVOURITE RECORDS

1. *Stella – Yello*
2. *In Strict Tempo – Dave Ball*
3. *The Idiot – Iggy Pop*

PREFERRED COMPANY ON DESERT ISLAND

Sigourney Weaver

MOST IRRITATING HABIT

Not having an irritating habit

FAVOURITE SHOP

Woolworths in Brixton

IDEAL NEXT PRIME MINISTER

Zippy the Pin Head

FAVOURITE BIRTHSIGN

My girlfriend's

FAVOURITE COMPUTER GAME

Fiddling my tax returns

FAVOURITE MOVIES

1. *I'm Gonna Get You Suckas*
2. *Heathers*
3. *Sex, Lies & Videotapes*

FAVOURITE OFF-DUTY PASTIMES

1. *Going to the Albert in Brixton*
2. *Ditto*
3. *Ditto*

LAST BOOK READ

'This Perfect Day' Ira Levin

FAVOURITE NEWSPAPER

Guardian

WHY?

Because I'm a Pinko Commie,
Bleeding Heart Liberal

FAVOURITE TV SHOW

The A Team

FAVOURITE FIGURE IN TERRAN HISTORY

Venus De Milo

She'd been feeding the scissorfish when it happened.

Tyranny had bought them from a skindealer in the Terraces, hypnotised by the way they changed colour. Press your hand against the glass and seconds later it would be Xeroxed onto the side of the fish in perfect 3D. They were a small novelty but they made the cheap apartment seem less cheap. She'd been in hiding for the last three months now, locked away on this cold nowhere planet with only a rack full of stim:cubes and a vibropak to pass the time. There was always SM-TV, the satellite snuff-channel, but she'd grown bored with that after twenty minutes. Only the fish held any real interest. They gathered mouth-up at the surface, like pieces of broken mirror. Careful of her fingers she lowered a strip of raw ghoti into the aquarium.

It was snowing heavily outside, Esquitou's bitter wind blowing fat white flakes into the window like spit. The voices of carol-singers drifted up from the street, lost, forlorn, desperate to be heard. Tyranny stopped and listened for a moment.

So praise our lord and martyr
The True God's word he sought
And from the depths of winter
A holy child brought forth.

She shrugged deeper into the kimono she was wearing, suddenly cold.

Martyrmas. Another yearly miracle; another yearly airing of sympathy and riches. She'd seen it before. The same lie on a hundred planets.

Outside the singing faltered and cut off in mid-word. Tyranny froze. Over the tapping of snow on glass she heard the understated *snakt* of bone. Then the screaming started.

She dashed to the window and looked out. Five floors below, on the tenement steps, something was butchering the carol-singers. Even as she watched she saw blood splash out across the snow, and the prayer-balloon one of the children had been holding drifted up past the window in front of her eyes.

A Tyranny Rex Story by **John Smith**
Art by **Duncan Fegredo**

SHADOWGROUND

There was a small bloody handprint smeared across it.

She saw everything – the flailing limbs, the terrified eyes, the wet shine of bone. But she couldn't see what was causing the carnage.

'It's invisible,' she heard herself say. 'Shule. It's *invisible.*'

Then she did see it. Or part of it. Outlined by a flurry of snow she caught the shape of its body, a fist the size of a dog. A rosette of fingers opened and closed, working bone and snow furiously into the palm of its mouth. For an instant a maze of yolk-yellow veins flared in the glass of its body, blinking on like dirty neon, and the demon changed. Changed *shape.* It collapsed inwards, spiralling into a cone, then unfolded itself like an origami flower. She knew instantly what she was looking at. It was a demon, an Asphyx, one of the brood-spawn from the lower Tiers. She'd seen them before – some of the spore-lords in the 4:Zone kept them as pets – but never one this big.

In the block across the street lights had come on, and people stood framed in the windows, staring down at the slaughter. The Asphyx moved, kicking up a storm of snow and meat, opening a ribcage like freshly-painted shutters. Tyranny slammed on the glass with her fists, screaming at the people in the street. *'Stop it! Why doesn't one of you* stop *it?'*

The demon paused, one glassy red paw clamped over a girl's screaming mouth, and looked up at her. She saw an anvil-shaped head swing up, its neck muscles rimmed with snow. Then it leapt, slammed up towards her like a locomotive, a vast colourless blur, streak of nothing against the falling snow.

Tyranny reeled back as the window exploded inwards, spraying her with glass. A fragment stuck in the soft flesh above her eye, and wetness ran down her face. The floor shuddered as the thing landed. A metre in front of her the floorboards rucked up into shavings.

She backed up against the wall, wind scrabbling for her under the silk kimono. Straining, she could just make out the Asphyx: the drizzle of water and blood on its hide – now smooth; now jagged as a broken bottle; now creased like a fevered man's bed sheets. And she could smell its breath, that cold iodine smell that went with all demons.

Then the wind changed, she glimpsed something flickering through the air, and the Asphyx hit her in the chest. It was soft and heavy and round, like a rotten beachfruit. Her skin opened as she reached for it, invisible switchblade nails slashing down from shoulder to elbow, unzipping her arm.

Pain slammed into her, scuttling along her nerves on fine wire legs, turning to lava in her head. Tyranny gritted her teeth and took a firmer hold of the demon. Her nails cut into it like peach-skin. It erupted in her hands in a flurry of shapes, trying to shake free. Bones braceletted her arms; grew mouths that nipped at her skin; buried gristle into the flesh of her breast. But she was determined not to let go.

Head spinning, Tyranny staggered to her feet and slammed her arm against the wall, as hard as she could. She did it again and again, until something inside the demon burst and the smell of iodine filled the air. For a second the coils around her wrist slackened, and she pulled the demon free with a gristly *shklukk.* Hardly thinking, she threw it into the aquarium.

Now it was in the water she could see it properly. It was like a bubble, a pocket of air that shivered through a kaleido-scope of shapes. Thrashing, it flung out four ape-like arms, scattering the scissorfish that had closed in on it, and started to haul itself out of the water.

Tyranny was standing by the ODO player, searching through the weapons in the module-belt. She looked up in time to see the Asphyx *change,* a spray of buzzsaws shrugging up from its back. Fish heads rained lazily down through the water.

Looks like another three months watching snuff-porn, she thought sourly, and pulled a blip-bomb off the belt. She thumbed the detonator and tossed it into the aquarium. It was like a furnace door being opened. Solid white light wiped away everything. The afterimage lingered for seconds, a giant white butterfly pinned on the front of her retinas.

Spitting blood, she tore a strip of

material from an old shirt and started to bandage her arm.

An hour later, and outside the city was possessed.

Tyranny shrugged deeper into her overjacket and tightened her grip on the snub-gun. She'd brought all the weapons she could carry – flechettes, zipsticks, limpet:50s, a Larsen genepak. This time she wanted to be prepared. But nothing had prepared her for this.

The demons where everywhere.

Some of them, like the Asphyx, were invisible: a squall of snow where there shouldn't be one; someone pinned to the ground by nothing, screaming as nothing took away his throat. But most

were only too visible. One, a cancer like an alcoholic's liver, had its organs hanging from its flanks and dragged them through the snow behind it. Another looked as if it had escaped from a Cubist's nightmare: it was eight feet tall, made out of squares of bone and gristle that constantly rearranged themselves as it moved, a Chinese puzzle desperately trying to solve itself.

There were more. And worse.

Wherever she looked there was destruction. Rickshaws and flivvercars lay overturned on the road; fire burned inside houses; demons jumped from roof to roof, sending snow sliding down into the street. Most of the people seemed to have made it indoors in time, but at every street corner she'd see another body hanging gutted from a traffic sign, or frozen to the sidewalk in its own blood.

She was coming into the Terraces now, expecting to find barricades; soldiers or MekTroops; at least med-squads clearing away the bodies. But it was the same as the outskirts. Snow and fire and the heady smell of iodine. Even the lights in the CRD precinct were off.

Up ahead the street was filled with the screeching of animals as a demon took one of the petmarts apart. Lutebirds and cockatoos fluttered out through the broken window, then seemed to stumble in mid-flight as they hit the cold.

Tyranny turned away and carried on, drawn by the unerring lizard instinct that yammered in its cage at the back of her head. It lead her through waterparks and forecourts, brightly-lit precincts littered with fresh fruit and corpses.

Ten minutes later she was there, cursing herself for not realising where she'd been heading:

The carnival.

It bulked up in the middle of the outfields like a giant chandelier, glass and chrome and light side-by-side with patched tents and garishly-painted caravans. A hologram danced and twisted in the darkness above the entranceway, a giant geisha twirling out the carnival's name in blue fire.

SHADOWGROUND

Tyranny stared up at the sign, her eyes turned to steel in the broken laserlight.

'Okay,' she said softly. 'Okay'.

She went in.

A carnival at high Martyrmas, the place would have normally been filled with life. But it was deserted, even of demons. Caught on the wind she heard the distant lilting music of a calliope, and felt suddenly lonely, a tiny fish lost in the guts of some sunken wreck.

Lights blinked, cheap neon jostling with lasers; hand-painted signs swung in and out of shadow. *The Cloud Garden. The Clockwork Zoo. Mephistopheles the Fire-Eater. The Torture Chamber of Hilda deSade.*

'You shouldn't have come here.'

Tyranny jerked round towards the voice. A man stood framed in the doorway of the *Water Maze*. His skin was black and shiny; his eyes were blacker, shinier. He was bald, the top of his head tattooed with thin blue lines like tribal scars. He wore the dark close-fitting suit of a preacher, but he had the build of a strongman. There was a whote rose pinned in his lapel. A hunch-backed dwarf crouched on a stool beside him. He was blind, eyes skimmed over with cataracts, but immaculately dressed: a check waistcoat, bow tie and white gloves.

Tyranny raised the snub-gun. 'What the hell *is* this?'

'It's *entertainment.* Thrills and spills. The smell of sawdust; the crack of the whip.' The black man gestured grandly. 'All good clean family fun.'

The dwarf giggled, saliva drooling down his chin. The black man plucked a handkerchief from empty air and wiped the spit away.

'Have you seen what's going *on* out there?' Tyranny demanded.

'Of course I have. I'm the showman.'

He moved forwards and Tyranny took an involuntary step back. The showman seemed puzzled by her reaction.

'Don't you know what night this is, child? This is Martyrmas Eve. Has no one told you the story? Of the martyr-king who went forth to seek the lord of all the world and unleashed dragons?'

Tyranny tightened her grip on the snub-gun. 'I'm not interested in fairy tales. I just want to know what the hell's going here.'

'This is the Siring. The Dread Birth.' The showman smiled; his teeth were flawlessly white and filed to points. 'You are at the beginning of the Age of Unreason.'

Somewhere above her there was a noise. Tyranny turned and saw something white and fleshy scuttling down the side of the tent towards her. Then the snub-gun was raised; spitting blue fire. Tyranny flipped backwards as the thing exploded, chunks of cooked albino meat raining around her.

Before she could get up the showman's hands had closed around her face. It took her totally by surprise. She lifted the snub-gun but the dwarf was suddenly *there*, teeth buried in the tendons of her wrist. Pinned down, all she could move was her tail. She lashed out blindly, and there was a sharp *snap* as it struck the showman's face. But he hardly seemed to notice. He was scrabbling at the insert-collar that jutted up at the base of her skull. That was the most vulnerable part of her. The jack-socket was linked directly to her central nervous system.

Tyranny twisted underneath him, trying to shake him free, but he had too tight a grip. He moved in quickly, his tongue darting over her neck, and she shivered as it touched the insert-socket. Then it was sliding in, branching out inside her, a net of nerves searching for

(contact he's trying to make contact)

a synapse point.

Desperate now, Tyranny concentrated all her strength into one violent lunge. Nails extended, she tore free from the dwarf's grip and reached up for the showman. A second before his tongue made contact she had his face in her hand. Her nails rose and fell, cutting like scalpels, and she felt skin slip easily from bone.

The showman jerked back, screaming, clutching the wound on his face. As Tyranny reached for the snub-gun the dwarf reared over her, drowning her in shadow. His hump had split open

and tiny hook-like hands were reaching from inside to widen the hole. Sickened, she turned the snub-gun and fired. The dwarf's insides splattered across the side of the tent in fat purple ropes. Whatever he'd given birth to scuttled mewling away into the dark.

She turned the snub-gun, ready to take out the showman, but he'd gone, leaving blood and a white rose behind.

Breathing raggedly, Tyranny climbed to her feet brushed herself down. The wounds in her arm had reopened, and her wrist was badly bruised, but otherwise she was unhurt. *Tough cookie*, she thought idly, and continued into the shadowground.

She passed razor games and

odoramas; gravity-chutes and sense-nets, all looking strangely dead now they weren't in use. As she left the lower quarters she saw a Marantz Dome, the words *Shape The Future* splashed across its rigging, a giant blister against the memoriless sky. Soon, though, she was in the upper quarters and the lasersprays had been replaced by Ferris Wheels and carousels and freakshows – things stolen from the history books. When she turned off the mainway and stumbled into the stadium she felt, for one hallucinatory moment, as if she'd stepped into the past.

Overhead the sky was snowblind, filled with the play of scatterlights from the lower quarters. It was a beautiful sight that made the thing in front of her seem even more *wrong*. She suddenly felt trapped in a fairy tale that had lost its way.

It arced up from the ground at the centre of the stadium, a flattened pentagonal hive the size of a house. Its walls were warped, uneven, and she might have thought they were made out of bark except for the way they rose and fell in a crude parody of breathing. Open sores wept at its base, showing a glimpse of the yellow fatty honeycombs within. Heavy black scaffolding, like the leftovers of an industrial revolution, grew up from the earth to form the pens, iron railings with barbed wire walls. They were filled with children. Tyranny guessed there were over a hundred, and though it was difficult to tell, none of them looked older than twelve.

Gathered round them, muzzles to the wire, were the demons. They crowded silently, patiently, waiting.

But what for? she asked herself.

There was movement at the edge of her vision and Tyranny saw the showman step out from behind the pens. He was following a tall fat man in a leather apron, hurrying to catch up with him. He looked like a butcher or a slaughterhouse worker. His arms were bare and bloody; knives gleamed in his belt. Even over the wind Tyranny could hear their voices. ▷

◁ 'But the bitch is still *out* there, Buer. Give me eight Asphyx. I'll take fledglings, if I have to. . . '

'We need all the Tier-brood for The Binding. How else do you expect us to draw Lansurisq from the Deeps?' He stopped and turned to the showman. 'No. If you need forces, use your own. Otherwise let me do my job.'

Tyranny watched the butcher turn and pad off towards the pens, the demons drawing back to let him through. She glanced at the showman. He was motionless, lost in thought. Then he shrugged. He reached into his jacket and pulled out a knife, doubled-edged, made of plexglass. He paused and looked nervously around him. His eyes were dark and haunted, and for an instant Tyranny thought she saw something human flicker through them. Then he seemed to make up his mind. He clasped both hands round the blade of the knife and squeezed hard, turning them in opposite directions like a man wringing water from a cloth. Blood welled up from between his fingers and poured into the sleet-grey dirt where it sizzled like oil on a skillet. Even from this distance Tyranny could see the droplets moving, clambering over each other in their haste to take on a form. They sucked up soil and sleet, moulding them into arms, legs, the nub of a head.

Within seconds the process was finished. Five dog-like creatures crouched there, pawing the ground. They were clubfooted, crude, unfinished, but they looked deadly. The showman held his hands out to them and the creatures took turns licking away the blood. He said something to them – too softly for her to hear what – and they leapt snorting into the night, bounding across the stadium with a grace that belied their appearance.

The showman wiped his face, exhausted. He pulled a handkerchief from nowhere and started bandaging his hands.

While he was occupied Tyranny took a sightfinder from her jacket and clipped it to the snub-gun. She searched his face, looking thought the scars to the man underneath, but there was nothing human there. She let the crosshairs come to rest on the bridge of his nose and, as the wind subsided, slowly squeezed the trigger. . .

Then a girl was screaming, and the shot went wide, turning a coin-sized square of girder to liquid. The showman carried on binding his hands, unaware of his escape. Tyranny lowered the snub-gun and scanned the pens, trying to pinpoint the sound. But coaxed by panic it had spread: everywhere she looked children were crying, screaming, clinging to each other like wreckage.

It was the butcher. He was working on the demons, moving what looked like a pneumatic drill between two of them as if carving off meat. There was a low chattering sound and suddenly they were *joined*, big black stitches running from shoulder to groin, knitting them together like Siamese twins. When the butcher leaned into the pen and dragged out a girl Tyranny knew at once what was happening.

He's going to sew them together. Children and demons. He's going to sew them together to make one body.

She remembered what the showman had said.

('the siring. the dread birth. the beginning of the age of unreason')

and imagined Lansurisq

(whatever it was whatever horror it was)

walking across the world in that terrible patchwork body, that huge quilted ragdoll of a body.

For a second she was too appalled to act. It was as if her mind was unable to fit around the idea and had broken into a dozen jagged pieces. Then adrenelin kicked in, and blind instinct took over. Tyranny was glad to give in to it.

With quick mechanical precision she removed the plasma:charge from the snub-gun and slotted in a clip of coil-cells. As she was lining up the sights she saw the butcher throw the girl over the back of one of the demons; hold her down with one hand; raise the drill. She had to get this right. If she was out by just a fraction of a degree she'd take the girl's head off.

She fired just as the drill started. There was a *shutt* of air and Tyranny saw the cell enter the butcher just below the ribcage. He froze, and for a second he seemed to stare straight at her, *into* her,

his eyes sad and lost and knowing. Then the cell exploded. It geysered up in a plume of surgical filament, hair-fine coil that twisted and writhed like snakes on coals. The butcher's body *vaporised* disappearing from the waist up in a fine red drizzle. His legs stood there for a moment, topless, then collapsed to their knees in the mud.

The girl had crawled away from the demons on her hands and knees and now, halfway across the stadium, she staggered to her feet and started running. Behind her the demons were fighting over the butcher's body. Others pawed the ground uneasily, glancing around the stadium. One of them set off after the girl in a drunken lolloping gait,

bile spurting from the gills in its neck. Tyranny fired the snub-gun again, turning it to pulp seconds before it reached her.

It must have been the smell of blood that started the panic. Soon the demons were lowing and shrieking like frightened cattle. Dozens broke into a stampede; others hurled themselves at the hive, blind in their desperation to escape.

Tyranny took advantage of the confusion. She dropped five of the demons with the snub-gun; another nine with limpets. All the time she was moving nearer to the pens, keeping to the shadows, praying the demons were too frightened or stupid to smell her. She could hear the children over the roar of hooves, a chorus of screams like a lunatic choir. The sound seemed to unnerve the demons even more. They gored each other open as they tried to get away from it as quickly as they could.

It was only when the ground started shuddering under her feet that Tyranny realised it wasn't the screaming that had scared them. Looking past the demons she saw the hive had ruptured, black rheum flooding from the sores at its base in a shiny clotted tide. It steamed in the cold air and Tyranny caught its smell, iodine undercut with something worse, something *far* worse.

What few demons there still were bolted, eyes wide, nostrils flaring with panic. It was coming, their Dread Lord Lansurisq, and it was not the courtly prince they had expected.

It was an atrocity.

And worse, it had no body.

The hive split with a sickening tearing sound, gaping red wounds spilling out the first traces of the Thriceborn. It was the colour of offal, of dead fat and gristle and crow pickings. As more of it came into view, hunched and wet and glistening, Tyranny began to perceive its shape. It was like a man bent at the waist, so low his head was touching his knees. A lance of bone transfixed it, running diagonally through thigh and neck, throwing antler-like spines out at ▷

angles through the body. But the skewer wasn't the relic of some ancient battle; it was *part* of the creature. The torso swivelled on it like some terrible slaughterhouse toy. Tyranny imagined it turning slowly in Hell, cooking in the brimstone heat like a joint on a spit, and felt sick to the pit of her stomach.

It wore rings through its throat, six of them rusted in place, and through the transparent skin of its back she could see the *things* inside it: animals shaped into organs; growths of coral with human faces; huge bitten tongues wrestling in lengths of gut. As she watched a slender headless neck twisted up from its back, like a swan's stripped down to muscle, and its tip blossomed into a bouquet of mouths.

Locked in the pens beneath it, the children were screaming, fighting to climb over the barbed wire, cutting their hands and feet to ribbons. A strip of lard-coloured flesh detached itself from Lansurisq's body and started stroking the children, trying to sooth them.

Hush, little ones, little dreamers. Hush, now.

Its mindvoice was soft, seductive, stealing through Tyranny like a drug. And didn't it sound *familiar*? Didn't it sound like her father, long dead now but who'd sung her to sleep as a baby?

She had to fight to shrug off its touch, coaxing her thoughts in a direction they didn't want to go. Then the ground was tilting under her, and she was in the air, a thigh-wide arm of gristle curled round her waist. She slashed out with her nails but its flesh parted under her, insubstantial as smoke.

Come nearer, child, that We might inspeckt you.

A sudden jolt sent the snub-gun spinning out of Tyranny's hand. Frightened now, *terrified*, she wrestled the zipstick out of her waistbelt and thumbed it on. The air solidified around its tip like water, a small shimmering pool.

You are Orphan, are you not? You are Orphan and We are Shaddowe, without shape, without body.

The thing around her waist threw off milky streamers that reached up towards her neck, feeling for the insert-socket there.

Would you not allowe us Entrie, child?

Tyranny was screaming in her head, shouting, cursing, trying to shrug out that ancient knowing mind as she sawed at her bonds with the zipstick. They started leaking thick white fluid and loosened suddenly, and she was falling. She hit the roof of the hive with enough impact to wind her. As she was struggling to her knees another limb stabbed down – this one fringed with teeth – and she twisted to avoid it.

Her mind was working furiously.

If Lansurisq had no body, was purely mind, spirit, soul (if demons had souls) then the hive was a doorway, and entrance to

(the deeps)

whatever insane place it had come from. Perhaps the hive was like a seed, setting down roots and sucking up food to knit new flesh for itself. If she could destroy *that*, shut *that* down. . .

She knew instantly what she had to do.

She pulled a stylet from the genepak in her waistbelt and unclipped the tail. Inside it was a sealed hypodermic, OPTIMUM ENVIRONMENT stencilled minutely down one side. She broke the seal and scraped the needle across the back of her hand, taking a tiny shaving of skin. As she was slotting the hypodermic back into the tail another offshoot came flailing towards her, bristling with steel-blue hairs. It missed her by inches. She dug her heels into the skin and crawled towards the centre of the hive. The roof was thin and membranous here, and slippery with resin. She searched with her fingers, feeling for the most vulnerable area, and planted the stylet in the soft damp skin. It was gone in an instant, disappearing into black flesh like a hot coal in snow.

The stylets were a medical development that had been taken over by the weaponsmiths. Originally they'd been used to inoculate soldiers against disease in the field. Now they were a routine part of genetic warfare. By modifying the source DNA they could turn the most benign cells to killers almost instantly.

She imagined the virus multiplying inside the hive, reeling out on its deadly spinning trajectory, and the word came

whispering up to Tyranny:

Cancer.

It had taken hold within seconds, urging young cells into malignant life, shrivelling muscle and nerve and wound raw tissue like fire. The malformed ribs that supported the hive heaved up through its skin as if they they were water-pipes in an earthquake, cancer bursting out from bone like bunches of black overripe grapes.

The hive yawned open beneath her, and Tyranny caught a glimpse of the bubbling yellow fat inside. She inched over to the edge of the hive, and digging her nails into the splitting flesh climbed quickly down its side. She was in one of the pens now, the children backing away

from her as if *she* was a demon. But when she'd blasted the barbed wire open they were eager to take advantage of the offer.

Above her, Lansurisq shuddered on its bone spire, looking now as if it actually *was* impaled. As Tyranny watched, its skin grew taunt and split, black-green ichor spraying out from deep ragged wounds. Lansurisq was a fuse, alight with cancer, decay clambering across its body like black fire. Opening the other pens, Tyranny ducked as ragged pieces of meat started to rain around her, fizzling to nothing as they hit the ground.

Then the demon was screaming, a booming thunderous scream that was big enough to shake the world. Tyranny clamped her hands over her ears; felt migraine sawing in her head. The children ran for the safety of the booths, hysterical with fear. Most of their noses were bleeding.

High on its spine Lansurisq was dwindling, folding inwards, collapsing into the wreckage of the hive like wet black ash. For one terrible moment she saw its organs – caught on the branching antlers that pierced its body – burst like water-filled balloons. Its skinned angle-poise neck snaked up, spitting from a dozen mouths as cancer stripped it down to cartilage.

It was over in minutes. The hive had become a ruin, a pile of offal steaming in the middle of the stadium. The stench of rotten meat and iodine filled the air, but it grew weaker as the wind razored in. Soon everything smelled of winter again.

Tyranny kicked through the clots of decay, searching for life, but there was nothing. She wiped sweat from her forehead with the palm of her hand, then walked over to the edge of the stadium where the children had gathered. There was sobbing, and tears; stranger hugging stranger. Tyranny stood with them in the shadows, looking up at that vast white sky.

'It's Martyrmas Day,' a child said somewhere, quietly.

Minutes later it was snowing. ○

2000 A.D. PROG 102. P23

I'M ABOARD! AMAZING- ME, ALEC TRENCH THE FAILURE, HAVING A CLOSE ENCOUNTER OF THE THIRD KIND! WHAT A STORY THIS WILL MAKE!
SWITCH OFF THE TRANSPORTER BEAM, NORIN. I'LL KILL THE EARTHLING AND BEGIN THE TESTS!
K-KILL ME? N-NOW WAIT JUST A MINUTE, FELLAS! I'M A GOOD UNION MAN-
THIS ONE IS DIFFERENT FROM THE OTHERS. SEE, HE HAS SOMETHING GROWING FROM HIS ANKLE!
PITY WE ALWAYS HAVE TO KILL THEM TO PREVENT ESCAPE. HE COULD BE A FINE LIVE SPECIMEN, NORIN-ESPECIALLY IF HE HAS ANY OTHER PECULIARITIES!
TRENCH THOUGHT FAST-
PECULIARITIES? I'LL GIVE 'EM PECULIARITIES!
OH I'M UNIQUE, I'M THE ONLY ONE LIKE ME! I CAN SING, I CAN DANCE-SHOOBIE DOOBIE DOO, SHOOBIE DOOBIE DEE.
THE ALIENS WERE INTRIGUED- AND TRENCH DIDN'T GIVE THEM TIME TO CHANGE THEIR MINDS!
LOOK, YOU GUYS, WHY DON'T WE MAKE A DEAL? I WON'T TRY TO ESCAPE, AND YOU CAN DO ANY TESTS ON ME YOU LIKE-AS LONG AS YOU SET ME FREE IN... SAY, A MONTH'S TIME...
A WILLING SPECIMEN AT LAST! AGREED, EARTHLING!
LET THE TESTS BEGIN AT ONCE!

THEIR TESTS WERE HELL—BUT TRENCH GRITTED HIS TEETH. IT WAS ONLY FOR A MONTH—AND WHEN HE GOT OUT OF THERE HE WAS GOING TO WRITE THE GREATEST SCI-FI STORY EVER!
HA, HA! P-PULLING ME TO PIECES! HAHAHA! GRIN AND BEAR IT, ALEC!
SKELETAL ELASTICITY 0.6%. SKIN SENSITIVITY UNIMPAIRED!
PAIN REFLEXES 98%. BONES FLATTEN AFTER SECOND BLOW!
AARGH!
AARGH!!
BY THE END OF THE MONTH TRENCH WAS STILL—MIRACULOUSLY—ALIVE...
FOR THE NEXT SERIES OF TESTS WE ARE GOING TO SUBJECT YOU TO SOME SEVERE ELECTRIC SHOCKS. DORMA, PREPARE THE MACHINE!
NOT SO FAST, BUDDY! THE MONTH'S UP—YOU GOTTA SET ME FREE NOW, LIKE YOU PROMISED!
THE MONTH IS UP? I FEAR THERE IS SOME MISUNDERSTANDING. EH, NORIN?
YES INDEED. ONE EARTH MONTH MIGHT BE OVER—BUT THE DELTA CENTAURAN MONTH IS EQUAL TO TEN OF YOUR EARTH YEARS! HAHA, YOU'RE NOT FREE YET!
THEY'VE TRICKED ME! I'LL NEVER STAND ANOTHER TEN YEARS OF TORTURE! I'VE GOT TO THINK OF SOMETHING FAST—
COME NOW, HUMAN, BE A GOOD SPORT AND LET NORIN ATTACH THE ELECTRODES!

W-WAIT A MINUTE... AT LEAST ALLOW ME ONE REQUEST! I'D LIKE TO TAKE SOME-SOME PHOTOGRAPHS OF YOU- FOR A STORY I'M GOING TO WRITE!
THAT SEEMS FAIR, DORMA!
YES, WE HAVE A CAMERA THE HUMAN CAN USE!
EZQUERRA
THE ALIENS WERE JUST LIKE MOST HUMANS- VAIN! THEY GOT CARRIED AWAY AS SOON AS A CAMERA WAS PRODUCED!
NOW, HOW ABOUT ME TAKING A SHOT OF THE TWO OF YOU TOGETHER? AN 'ALIEN SCIENTISTS AT WORK' SORT OF THING! HERE, STAND BY YOUR MACHINE-MAKE IT LOOK REALISTIC!
THIS IS FUN!
HOW'S THIS?
BE SURE TO GET MY GOOD SIDE, HUMAN!
BEAUTIFUL! IT'S ALMOST... TOO EASY! JUST GIVE ME A BIG SMILE...
FULL POWER
OFF

...AND SAY "AIEEEE!"
AIEEEEE!
FULL POWER
OFF
HA HA! I BEAT YOU AT YOUR OWN GAME, YOU SPACE RATS!
TRENCH SAT DOWN RIGHT THERE AND WROTE HIS STORY. HE WANTED EVERY DETAIL FRESH-
YES, YES, THAT'S RICH! THARG'LL LOVE THE BIT ABOUT NORIN BREAKING MY NOSE!
WHEN THE STORY WAS FINISHED, TRENCH ADJUSTED THE BEAM TRANSPORTER-
I'LL FIX THIS THING SO I APPEAR RIGHT IN THARG'S OFFICE! THEN HE'LL KNOW I'VE GOT SOMETHING HOT!
GOODBYE, FELLAS. YOU GAVE ME A MONTH OF HELL, BUT IT WAS WORTH IT! I'LL BE THE BIGGEST NAME IN SCI-FI!

POOR ALEC TRENCH. HE COULD NEVER GET **ANYTHING** RIGHT!
H-HOLY HAMISH! I-I MUST HAVE SET THE CO-ORDINATES WRONG!
MR THARG, SIR- ISN'T THAT **ALEC TRENCH?**
HEEELP!
HMMM... YES, IT DOES LOOK LIKE HIM!
YES, THAT'S ALEC TRENCH ALL RIGHT! WONDER WHY HE DIDN'T DROP IN FOR A CHAT?
THAT LOOKS LIKE AN ENVELOPE FLUTTERING DOWN!
IT'S ADDRESSED TO YOU, SIR!
HMMPH! SOME WRITERS WILL TRY **ANYTHING** TO GET A STORY ACCEPTED!
THARG
WELL, ALEC TRENCH DID GET A STORY ACCEPTED AFTER ALL. PITY HE COULDN'T HAVE BEEN AROUND TO SEE IT IN PRINT, THOUGH!
POOR BLIGHTER! THEY SAY HE WORKED FOR THAT STRANGE MR THARG ON THE TWENTIETH FLOOR!
WOULDN'T SURPRISE ME IF HE DID, DUCKS. AIN'T NOTHING BEEN SAFE AROUND HERE SINCE HIM AND THEM ROBOTS MOVED IN!
THE END

THE 2000 AD INDEX

Just what you always needed! A complete comprehensive index to every series that's ever run in the Galaxy's Greatest Comic. The information is laid out so as to cause minimum confusion.

Judge Dredd has been indexed before in the **Judge Dredd Annual** for 1988, and **Future Shocks** will be indexed sometime in the near future. Now, you're on your own!

A.B.C. Warriors

Title: A.B.C. Warriors.
Progs 119-139.
From 30/06/79 to 17/11/79.
21 Eps. 129 pages.
Script: Pat Mills.
Art: O'Neill/McCarthy/McMahon/Ewins/Gibbons/Ezquerra.

Title: A.B.C. Warriors Book 2.
Progs 555-581.
From 02/01/88 to 02/07/88.
21 Eps. 133 pages.
Script: Pat Mills.
Art: Bisley/sms.

Ace Trucking Co.

Title: Ace Trucking Co.
Progs 232-236.
From 03/10/81 to 31/10/81.
5 Eps. 25 pages.
Script: Wagner/Grant.
Art: Massimo Belardinelli.

Title: Hell's Pocket.
Progs 239-243.
From 21/11/81 to 19/12/81.
5 Eps. 20 pages.
Script: Wagner/Grant.
Art: Ian Gibson.

Title: Lugjack.
Progs 244-250.
From 26/12/81 to 06/02/82.
7 Eps. 35 pages.
Script: Wagner/Grant.
Art: Massimo Belardinelli.

Title: Great Mush Rush, The.
Progs 251-258.
From 13/02/82 to 03/04/82.
8 Eps. 42 pages.
Script: Wagner/Grant.
Art: Massimo Belardinelli.

Title: Ughbug Bloos, The.
Progs 259.
From 10/04/82.
1 Eps. 4 pages.
Script: Wagner/Grant.
Art: Massimo Belardinelli.

Title: Joobaloo.
Progs 268-272.
From 12/06/82 to 10/07/82.
5 Eps. 25 pages.
Script: Wagner/Grant.
Art: Massimo Belardinelli.

Title: Too Many Bams.
Progs 273-278.
From 17/07/82 to 21/08/82.
6 Eps. 31 pages.
Script: Wagner/Grant.
Art: Massimo Belardinelli.

Title: Kloistar Run, The.
Progs 279-285.
From 28/08/82 to 09/10/82.
7 Eps. 35 pages.
Script: Wagner/Grant.
Art: Massimo Belardinelli.

Title: Stoop Coop Soup.
Progs 288-293.
From 30/10/82 to 04/12/82.
6 Eps. 30 pages.

A.B.C. Warriors

Ace Trucking Co.

Adventures of Luke Kirby

Anderson Psi Division

Script: Wagner/Grant.
Art: Massimo Belardinelli.

Title: On the Dangle.
Progs 378-386.
From 11/08/84 to 06/09/84.
9 Eps. 45 pages.
Script: Wagner/Grant.
Art: Massimo Belardinelli.

Title: Strike!
Progs 387-400.
From 13/10/84 to 12/01/85.
13 Eps. 64 pages.
Script: Wagner/Grant.
Art: Massimo Belardinelli.

Title: Doppelgarp, The.
Progs 451-472.
From 04/01/86 to 31/05/86.
22 Eps. 87 pages.
Script: Wagner/Grant.
Art: Massimo Belardinelli.

Title: Garpetbaggers, The.
Progs 475-498.
From 21/06/86 to 29/11/86.
24 Eps. 94 pages.
Script: Wagner/Grant.
Art: Massimo Belardinelli.

Adventures of Luke Kirby

Title: Summer Magic.
Progs 571-577.
From 23/04/88 to 04/06/88.
7 Eps. 36 pages.
Script: Alan McKenzie.
Art: John Ridgway.

Anderson Psi Division

Title: Four Dark Judges.
Progs 416-427.
From 04/05/85 to 20/07/85.
12 Eps. 62 pages.
Script: Wagner/Grant.
Art: Ewins/Robinson.

Title: Possessed, The.
Progs 468-478.
From 03/05/86 to 12/07/86.
11 Eps. 57 pages.
Script: Wagner/Grant.
Art: Brett Ewins.

Title: Hour of the Wolf.
Progs 520-531.
From 02/05/87 to 18/07/87.
12 Eps. 62 pages.
Script: Wagner/Grant.
Art: Kitson/Simpson.

Title: Contact.
Progs 607-609.
From 31/12/88 to 14/01/89.
3 Eps. 15 pages.
Script: Alan Grant.
Art: Mark Farmer.

Title: Beyond the Void.
Progs 612-613.
From 04/02/89 to 11/02/89.
2 Eps. 10 pages.
Script: Alan Grant.
Art: Mick Austin.

Title: Helios.
Progs 614-622.
From 18/02/89 to 15/04/89.
9 Eps. 46 pages.
Script: Alan Grant.
Art: David Roach.

Title: Triad.
Progs 635-644.
From 15/07/89 to 16/09/89.
10 Eps. 50 pages.
Script: Alan Grant.
Art: Arthur Ranson.

Title: Prophet, The.
Progs 645-647.
From 23/09/89 to 07/10/89.
3 Eps. 17 pages.
Script: Alan Grant.
Art: David Roach.

Title: Random Man, The.
Progs 657-659.
From 16/12/89 to 30/12/89.
3 Eps. 15 pages.
Script: Alan Grant.
Art: Carlos Ezquerra.

Angel

Title: Angel.
Progs 95-99.
From 13/01/79 to 10/02/79.
5 Eps. 24 pages.
Script: Chris Stevens.
Art: Carlos Pino.

Ant Wars

Title: Ant Wars.
Progs 71-85.
From 01/07/78 to 07/10/78.
15 Eps. 83 pages.
Script: Gerry Finlay-Day.
Art: Ferrer/Azpiri.

Bad City Blue

Title: Bad City Blue.
Progs 468-477.
From 03/05/86 to 05/07/86.
10 Eps. 50 pages.
Script: Alan Grant.
Art: Robin Smith.

Bad Company

Title: Bad Company.
Progs 500-519.
From 13/12/86 to 25/04/87.
20 Eps. 118 pages.
Script: Pete Milligan.
Art: Ewins J. McCarthy.

Title: Bad Company II
The Bewilderness.
Progs 548-585.
From 14/11/87 to 30/07/88.
20 Eps. 123 pages.
Script: Pete Milligan.
Art: Ewins J. McCarthy.

Title: Simply.
Progs 601.
From 19/11/88.
1 Eps. 4 pages.
Script: Pete Milligan.
Art: Ewins/Dillon.

Angel

Ant Wars

Bad Company

Beyond Zero

Beyond Zero

Title: Beyond Zero Part 1.
Progs 630-634.
From 10/06/89 to 08/07/89.
5 Eps. 25 pages.
Script: John Brosnan.
Art: Kev Hopgood.

Title: Beyond Zero Part 2.
Progs 645-649.
From 23/09/89 to 21/10/89.
5 Eps. 25 pages.
Script: John Brosnan.
Art: Kev Hopgood.

Blackhawk

Title: Blackhawk.
Progs 127-161.
From 25/08/79 to 19/04/80.
34 Eps. 152 pages.
Script: Alan Grant.
Art: Massimo Belardinelli.

Bonjo from Beyond the Stars

Title: Bonjo from Beyond the Stars.
Progs 41-49.
From 03/12/77 to 04/02/78.
9 Eps. 43 pages.
Script: Kev O'Neill.
Art: Kev O'Neill.

Bradley

Title: Alternators™ (Future Shock).
Progs 533.
From 01/08/87.
1 Eps. 2 pages.
Script: Alan McKenzie.
Art: Simon Harrison.

Title: Bradley's Birthday.
Progs 545.
From 24/10/87.
1 Eps. 3 pages.
Script: Alan McKenzie.
Art: Simon Harrison.

Title: Bradley and the Bandit.
Progs 552.
From 12/12/87.
1 Eps. 5 pages.
Script: Alan McKenzie.
Art: Simon Harrison.

Title: Bradley's Xmas.
Progs 554.
From 26/12/87.
1 Eps. 4 pages.
Script: Alan McKenzie.
Art: Simon Harrison.

Title: Bradley & The Toboggan Race.
Progs 606.
From 24/12/88.
1 Eps. 4 pages.
Script: Alan McKenzie.
Art: Simon Harrison.

Captain Klep

Title: Captain Klep.
Progs 127-159.
From 25/08/79 to 08/03/80.
18 Eps. 18 pages.
Script: Dave Angus/Stevens.
Art: O'Neill/Ailie/Willow/Rob Smith.

Chopper

Title: Soul on Fire.
Progs 594-597.
From 01/10/88 to 22/10/88.
4 Eps. 27 pages.
Script: John Wagner.
Art: Colin MacNeil.

Colony Earth

Title: Colony Earth.
Progs 52-61.
From 18/02/78 to 22/04/78.
10 Eps. 41 pages.
Script: Jim Watson.
Art: Jim Watson.

D.R. & Quinch

Title: D.R. & Quinch Have Fun On Earth.
Progs 317.
From 21/05/83.
1 Eps. 6 pages.
Script: Alan Moore.
Art: Alan Davis.
Reprinted: Best of 2000 AD Monthly 8.

Title: D.R. & Quinch Go Straight.
Progs 350-351.
From 07/01/84 to 14/01/84.
2 Eps. 12 pages.
Script: Alan Moore.
Art: Alan Davis.
Reprinted: Best of 2000 AD Monthly 17.

Title: D.R. & Quinch Go Girl Crazy.
Progs 352-354.
From 21/01/84 to 04/02/84.
3 Eps. 15 pages.
Script: Alan Moore.
Art: Alan Davis.
Reprinted: Best of 2000 AD Monthly 17.

Title: D.R. & Quinch Get Drafted.
Progs 355-359.
From 11/02/84 to 10/03/84.
5 Eps. 24 pages.
Script: Alan Moore.
Art: Alan Davis.
Reprinted: Best of 2000 AD Monthly 18.

Title: D.R. & Quinch Go to Hollywood.
Progs 363-367.
From 07/04/84 to 05/05/85.
5 Eps. 25 pages.
Script: Alan Moore.
Art: Alan Davis.
Reprinted: Best of 2000 AD Monthly 19.

Blackhawk

Bonjo from Beyond the Stars

Bradley

Captain Klep

Title: D.R. & Quinch's Agony Page.
Progs 525-534.
From 06/06/87 to 08/08/87.
9 Eps. 9 pages.
Script: Jamie Delano.
Art: Alan Davis/Mark Farmer.

Dan Dare

Title: Dan Dare.
Progs 1-11.
From 26/02/77 to 07/05/77.
11 Eps. 55 pages.
Script: Kelvin Gosnell.
Art: Massimo Belardinelli.

Title: Hollow World.
Progs 12-23.
From 14/05/77 to 30/07/77.
12 Eps. 65 pages.
Script: Steve Moore.
Art: Massimo Belardinelli.

Title: Legion.
Progs 28-33.
From 03/09/77 to 08/10/77.
5 Eps. 31 pages.
Script: Gerry Finlay-Day.
Art: Dave Gibbons.

Title: Greenworld.
Progs 34-35.
From 15/10/77 to 22/10/77.
2 Eps. 10 pages.
Script: Gerry Finlay-Day.
Art: Dave Gibbons.

Title: Star Slayer.
Progs 36-51.
From 29/10/77 to 11/02/78.
24 Eps. 63 pages.
Script: Gerry Finlay-Day.
Art: Dave Gibbons.

Title: Doppelganger.
Progs 52-55.
From 18/02/78 to 11/03/78.
4 Eps. 17 pages.
Script: Chris Lowder.
Art: Dave Gibbons.

Title: Waterworld.
Progs 56-60.
From 18/03/78 to 15/04/78.
5 Eps. 22 pages.
Script: Chris Lowder.
Art: Dave Gibbons.

Title: Nightmare.
Progs 61-63.
From 22/04/78 to 06/05/78.
3 Eps. 12 pages.
Script: Chris Lowder.
Art: Brian Lewis.

Title: Ice World.
Progs 64-66.
From 13/05/78 to 27/05/78.
3 Eps. 12 pages.
Script: Gerry Finlay-Day.
Art: Dave Gibbons.

Title: Garden of Eden.
Progs 67-72.
From 03/06/78 to 08/07/78.
6 Eps. 29 pages.
Script: Chris Lowder.
Art: Dave Gibbons.

Title: Mutiny.
Progs 73-78.
From 15/07/78 to 19/08/78.
6 Eps. 27 pages.
Script: Chris Lowder.
Art: Dave Gibbons.

Title: The Doomsday Machine.
Progs 79-85.
From 26/08/78 to 07/10/78.
7 Eps. 40 pages.
Script: Landau/Preston.
Art: Goring/Leech.

Title: Servant of Evil.
Progs 100-126.
From 17/02/79 to 18/08/79.
26 Eps. 128 pages.
Script: Tom Tully.
Art: Dave Gibbons.

Dash Decent

Title: Dash Decent.
Progs 178-198.
From 20/09/80 to 07/02/81.
20 Eps. 21 pages.
Script: Angus/O'Neill.
Art: Kev O'Neill.

Dead, The

Title: Dead, The.
Progs 510-519.
From 21/02/87 to 25/04/87.
10 Eps. 49 pages.
Script: Pete Milligan.
Art: Massimo Belardinelli.

Death Planet

Title: Death Planet.
Progs 62-70.
From 29/04/78 to 24/06/78.
9 Eps. 40 pages.
Script: Alan Hebden.
Art: Lopez.

Disaster 1990

Title: Disaster 1990.
Progs 119-139.
From 30/06/79 to 17/11/79.
21 Eps. 104 pages.
Script: Gerry Finlay-Day.
Art: Carlos Pino.

Fervent and Lobe.

Title: Issigri Variations.
Progs 642-649.
From 02/09/89 to 21/10/89.
8 Eps. 33 pages.
Script: John Smith.
Art: Mike Hadley.

Fiends of the Eastern Front

Title: Fiends of the Eastern Front.
Progs 152-161.

Chopper

D.R. & Quinch

Dan Dare

Dash Decent

From 16/02/80 to 19/04/80.
10 Eps. 44 pages.
Script: Gerry Finlay-Day.
Art: Carlos Ezquerra.

Flesh

Title: Flesh Book 1.
Progs 1-19.
From 26/02/77 to 02/07/77.
19 Eps. 87 pages.
Script: Pat Mills.
Art: Sola/Boix/Carrion.
2000 AD Annual 82/84/89.

Title: Flesh Book 2.
Progs 86-99.
From 14/10/78 to 10/02/79.
8 Eps. 78 pages.
Script: Roy Preston.
Art: Massimo Belardinelli.

Freaks

Title: Freaks.
Progs 542-547.
From 03/10/87 to 07/11/87.
6 Eps. 30 pages.
Script: Pete Milligan.
Art: John Higgins.

Halo Jones

Title: Ballad of Halo Jones: Book 1.
Progs 376-385.
From 07/07/84 to 29/09/84.
10 Eps. 51 pages.
Script: Alan Moore.
Art: Ian Gibson.
Reprinted: Best of 2000 AD No 40.

Title: Ballad of Halo Jones: Book 2.
Progs 406-415.
From 23/02/85 to 27/04/85.
10 Eps. 56 pages.
Script: Alan Moore.
Art: Ian Gibson.
Reprinted: Best of 2000 AD No 42.

Title: Ballad of Halo Jones: Book 3.
Progs 451-466.
From 04/01/86 to 19/04/89.
15 Eps. 80 pages.
Script: Alan Moore.
Art: Ian Gibson.

Hap Hazard

Title: Hap Hazzard (Future Shock).
Progs 561.
From 13/02/88.
1 Eps. 4 pages.
Script: Steve Dillon.
Art: Steve Dillon.

Title: Hap Hazzard 2.
Progs 567.
From 26/03/88.
1 Eps. 3 pages.
Script: Steve Dillon.
Art: Steve Dillon.

Title: Hap Hazzard 3.
Progs 588.
From 20/08/88.
1 Eps. 5 pages.
Script: Steve Dillon.
Art: Steve Dillon.

Title: Hap Hazzard 4: Life. . .
Progs 609.
From 14/01/89.
1 Eps. 4 pages.
Script: Steve Dillon.
Art: Steve Dillon.

Title: Hap Hazzard 5.
Progs 610.
From 21/01/89.
1 Eps. 5 pages.
Script: Steve Dillon.
Art: Steve Dillon.

Harlem Heroes

Title: Harlem Heroes.
Progs 1-27.
From 26/02/77 to 27/08/77.
27 Eps. 112 pages.
Script:
Art: Dave Gibbons.

Harry 20 on the High Rock

Title: Harry 20 on the High Rock
Progs 287-307.
From 23/10/82 to 12/03/83.
21 Eps. 106 pages.
Script: Gerry Finlay-Day.
Art: Alan Davis.
Reprinted: Best of 2000 AD Monthly 27/28.

Hell Trekkers

Title: Hell Trekkers.
Progs 387-415.
From 13/10/84 to 27/04/85.
29 Eps. 120 pages.
Script: Wagner/Grant.
Art: Jose Ortiz.

Inferno

Title: Inferno.
Progs 36-75.
From 29/10/77 to 29/07/78.
40 Eps. 183 pages.
Script: Tom Tully.
Art: Massimo Belardinelli.

Invasion

Title: Invasion.
Progs 1-51.
From 26/02/77 to 11/02/78.
51 Eps. 234 pages.
Script: Gerry Finlay-Day.
Art: Carlos Pino.

continued on page 75

Disaster 1990

Fervent and Lobe.

THE NU EARTH FUTURE WAR. ROGUE TROOPER IS IN THE DESERT CITY OF KYRO, IN THE FOUL-AIRED ALIEN QUARTER KNOWN AS THE 'GASBAH'. BUT, THOUGH ON THE RUN, HE IS AN UNWELCOME GUEST...
GUESS I'LL SPEND THE NIGHT HERE. GOT A ROOM FOR ME, BAR-MAN?
RIX BAH
YOU'RE MAKING A BIG MISTAKE, G.I.
THERE WERE ONLY A HANDFUL OF HUMANS IN THE GASBAH, LIKE THE CHEMICALLY-DISABLED BARMAN...
GOT ANY MONEY? NO MONEY, NO ROOM!
BAGMAN?
COMIN' UP, ROGUE.
ROGUE TROOPER
THE GASBAH —— Part TWO
ROGUE'S BIO-CHIPPED PACK DISPENSED A GLINTING OBJECT...
GOLD MICROBAR— FROM THE SURVIVAL KIT! GUESS THAT WILL COVER THE RENT, HUH?
2000 A.D. Credit Card:
SCRIPT ROBOT GERRY FINLEY-DAY
ART ROBOT CAM KENNEDY
LETTERING ROBOT BILL NUTTALL
COMPU-73E
THE BARMAN GRUDGINGLY ACCEPTED THE PAYMENT.
BUY A GIRL A SYNTHI-DRINK, BIG BOY?
THE BAR'S BUBBLE DANCER. A HUMAN GIRL ENTERTAINER WORKING THE GASBAH.

DAMES AND GIs DON'T MIX, ROGUE — REMEMBER YOUR TRACK RECORD.
SISTER SLEDGE, VENUS BLUEGENES...
OHH — SYNTHESIZED VOICES! WHAT ARE THEY SAYING?
GIVIN' ME SOME TIMELY ADVICE, MA'AM. BARMAN, GET THE LADY A DRINK THEN SHOW ME TO MY ROOM.
AN ALIEN PORTER CAME FORWARD...
I TAKE-A YOUR BAG?
LEAVE ME BE, ALI.
'ALI'—ARMY TERM FOR ALIEN.
HERE WE ARE, SIR— ROOM EIGHT
OOPS! SO SORRY, SIR. I FORGOT IT'S— AH, OCCUPIED BY A GUEST FROM THE SPROL SYSTEM, WHO ALSO HAS ROOMS SIX AND SEVEN.
THEN —
AH, YOUR ROOM AT LAST, SIR.
GREAT— BE A CHANGE FROM SLEEPIN' OUT IN THE FIELD.
BUT BELOW...
THE G.I. IS IN THAT ROOM. HAVE YOU YOUR BEAST READY?
DAS— DAS.

REMEMBER HE IS IMMUNE TO MOST POISONS OF NU EARTH, BUT PERHAPS NOT YOUR HOME-PLANET TOXINS...
DAS.
LATER...
BOY, SOME JOINT. THOSE MINOR LIFE-FORMS I'M PICKING UP MUST BE BED-BUGS!
QUIET! MY SENSOR'S PICKING UP A BIGGER LIFE-FORM... **MUCH** BIGGER!
HEY, ROGUE!
HUH?
HELL! **ALI SNAKE!** GUNNAR—GET READY!
I'LL BRING IT INTO YOUR SIGHTS!
READY!
KLIK!
THE BIO-CHIPPED ASSAULT RIFLE OPENED UP...
HSSSSSSS!
HSSS!
HSSS!

THEN...
SOME HEAD COUNT, HUH?
SOMEONE RUNNING DOWN THE ALLEY OUT-SIDE!
ROGUE LEAPT FROM HIS WINDOW...
HOLD IT, ALI!
SHEK!
FINALLY, THE ALIEN WAS CORNERED...
NOW YOU'RE GONNA TELL ME WHO GOT YOU TO DO YOUR SNAKE ACT.
HAS NE!
WAS IT YOUR IDEA? WHO'S GOT IT IN FOR ME IN THE GASBAH? TELL ME!
EASY, ROGUE HE'LL TALK—WE NEED BAGMAN TO TRANSLATE.
DAS!
SUDDENLY...
HSSSSSAAA!
THTUNK!

HE'S BEEN SILENCED! AND BY A NORT WEAPON! SOMETHING THE ALIS PICKED UP—OR COULD THERE BE ENEMY AGENTS IN THE GASBAH? IF SO, WHAT'S THEIR GAME SO FAR FROM THE FRONT?
A HUNDRED CLICKS AWAY OUT IN THE WILDERNESS WEST OF KYRO...
THIS HAD BETTER BE IMPORTANT —SWITCHING ME OUT OF MY HYPO-SLEEP!
YES, GENERAL. SIGNAL FROM OUR RING IN THE KYRO GASBAH!
THE G.I. THERE, OF ALL PEOPLE! HE COULD WRECK OUR WHOLE PLAN!
YESSIR. I IMMEDIATELY CONTACTED SCI-INT!
'SCI-INT': SCIENTIFIC INTELLIGENCE.
FROM NORT LINES RACED A STAMEL—A GENETICALLY ENGINEERED DESERT CREATURE...
A RIDER IS ALREADY ON HIS WAY WITH THE WEAPON. TOMORROW, D-DAY, WILL BE DOOMS-DAY FOR THE G.I.!
THEN THE GASBAH, KYRO AND THIS WHOLE DESERT ZONE IS OURS!
KYRO
TIMBUK 2

DROIDS LIFESTYLE QUESTIONNAIRE

DESIGNATION *Lettering Droid*
Kid Robson

FAVOURITE 2000 AD STORY
He Met The Moonmen

FAVOURITE FOODS
1. *Fish & Chips*
2. *Chicken & Chips*
3. *Pie & Chips*

FAVOURITE RECORDS
1. *Jim Reeves 12 Songs of Xmas*
2. *Classical & easy listening*
3. *John Barry Bond Soundtracks*

PREFERRED COMPANY ON DESERT ISLAND
Debee Ashby/Martine Beswick
(can I have both, please?)

MOST IRRITATING HABIT
Being perfect

FAVOURITE SHOP
Chip shop

IDEAL NEXT PRIME MINISTER
Dougal from the Magic Roundabout

FAVOURITE BIRTHSIGN
*Scorpio (we're the b*s*a*d* of the astrological world), (not that I believe in that sort of stuff, you understand.)*

FAVOURITE COMPUTER GAME
Computer? Are you kidding? On what Tharg pays?

FAVOURITE MOVIES
1. *An Inspector Calls*
2. *The Searchers*
3. *A Man Called Flintstone*

FAVOURITE OFF-DUTY PASTIMES
1. *Collecting comics*
2. *Collecting books*
3. *Collecting records & tapes*

LAST BOOK READ
The Penguin Kenneth Grahame

FAVOURITE NEWSPAPER
The Daily Record

WHY?
Programmes & cartoons pages

FAVOURITE TV SHOW
The Likely Lads

FAVOURITE FIGURE IN TERRAN HISTORY
Bob Hope (I've met him)

LOST IN ZERO
ZERO CITY AT NIGHT IS NO PLACE FOR A LITTLE BOY TO BE WANDERING AROUND ON HIS OWN.
VROOM!
2000 AD
SCRIPT JOHN BROSNAN
ART KEV HOPGOOD
LETTERING KID ROBSON
HELLO, WHAT'S THIS..?
SCREEECH!
HEY, KID, WHAT ARE YOU DOING OUT HERE IN THE STREET ?
YOU LIVE AROUND HERE, KID, OR ARE YOU LOST ?
YEAH, I'M LOST.
WELL, AT LEAST YOU CAN TALK. GUESS I'D BETTER TURN YOU OVER TO THE RENTACOPS.

WHAT'S YOUR NAME, KID?
LEROY. AND MY TEDDY'S NAME IS BRUCE.
HI LEROY. HI BRUCE. MY NAME IS TANNER.
HOTEL
RENTACOPS INC
HEY, HOLD IT, WILLYA!? I KNOW I GOT IT ON ME SOMEWHERE...!
HERE, I TOLD YOU I HAD IT. MY CREDIT DISC...
THAT'LL DO NICELY, SIR.
...THE KID'S LOST? SURE, WE'LL TAKE CARE OF HIM. BUT IT WILL COST YOU FOUR HUNDRED.
FOUR HUNDRED? THAT'S CRAZY!
NO, IT'S THE CURRENT RENTACOP FEE FOR THE LOCATING OF MISSING CHILDREN.
BUT I'VE ALREADY FOUND HIM! ALL YOU'VE GOT TO DO IS RETURN HIM TO HIS FOLKS!
SAME DIFFERENCE. BUT YOU CAN PROBABLY CLAIM THE MONEY BACK FROM HIS PARENTS.
I WOULDN'T HAVE THE NERVE. SO LONG, SISTER.

SO WHAT AM I GOING TO DO WITH YOU NOW, KID? ANY IDEAS?
KID..?
LEROY! WHERE ARE YOU!?
LEROY!
...GO ON, BRUCE, SAY HELLO TO THE NICE DOGGY...
UH OH...
SPLATT!
ZZAAPP!

YOU KILLED THE NICE DOGGY.
EITHER YOU'VE GOT DUD EYESIGHT, KID, OR YOU HAVE SOME REALLY STRANGE PETS AT YOUR HOUSE.
I'LL TAKE YOU OVER TO ALLANA'S PLACE...MAYBE SHE'LL HAVE SOME IDEA ON WHAT I CAN DO WITH YOU...
...AND THAT'S THE SITUATION, ALLANA. HE DOESN'T KNOW HIS ADDRESS AND THE RENTACOPS WANT A SMALL FORTUNE TO TAKE HIM OFF MY HANDS.
POOR LITTLE LAD. HE'S SO **SWEET**.
YOU LIKE HIM SO MUCH **YOU** TAKE CARE OF HIM FROM HERE ON.
DON'T BE SO MEAN, TANNER. YOU'LL HURT HIS FEELINGS.
OHHH!
WHAT'S THE MATTER ?
I DON'T BELIEVE IT ! THE LITTLE BRAT **GOOSED** ME !
THAT SWEET LITTLE ANGEL ? YOU MUST BE IMAGINING THINGS.

I KNOW WHEN I'VE BEEN GOOSED, TANNER, AND HE JUST GOOSED ME.
SURE...SURE. LOOK, I NEED HELP HERE. YOU GOT ANY IDEAS HOW I'M GOING TO UNLOAD HIM BACK ON HIS PARENTS?
WELL...MAYBE IF YOU JUST DRIVE HIM AROUND ZERO CITY UNTIL HE SPOTS SOME-THING FAMILIAR... LIKE WHERE HE LIVES.
GREAT. THAT COULD TAKE ALL NIGHT...AND YOU KNOW HOW LONG THE NIGHT IS IN ZERO CITY.
THIS NEIGHBOURHOOD LOOK LIKE HOME, KID?
NOPE.
FUNNY. I KNEW YOU WERE GOING TO SAY THAT.
SYNTH X
THERE! THERE!
AT LAST...
IF YOU LIVE HERE, KID, YOU HAVE MY SYMPATHY.
THE JOINT SURE IS JUMPING.

COME ON, KID, YOU MADE A MISTAKE. NOTHING'S LIVED HERE FOR YEARS...
SKREEEEEEE!
RUN KID! YOU'VE LED US INTO A NEST OF BAT-FREAKS!
SKREEEEEEE!
SKREEEEEEEE!
SKREEEEEEE!
I SAID RUN, KID!
GO GET 'EM, BRUCE.

SWISHHHH!
SKREEEEEE!
SWISHHH!
SKREEEEEE!
SWISHHH!
SKREEEEEE!
SWISHHH!
TEDDY BEARS HAVE SURE CHANGED SINCE I WAS A KID.
CRUMMPP!

WELL, I GUESS THE FUN'S OVER FOR TONIGHT, TANNER. I LIVE AT THE PHILIP K. DICK TOWER. APT # 309. TAKE ME THERE. YOU WILL BE REWARDED.
I'D BETTER BE, KID.
YEAH, WHAT DO YOU WANT ?
I HAVE SOMEBODY HERE WHO I THINK BELONGS TO YOU—YOUR SON.
DADDY ! YOU'RE BACK !
HI, BUBBLES, MISS ME ?
DADDY ?
DADDY IS JUST MY NICKNAME FOR HIM. ACTUALLY HE'S MY HUSBAND. ROLAND VAN PEETERS. PROBABLY THE RICHEST MAN IN ZERO CITY.
KIND OF SMALL FOR HIS AGE, ISN'T HE ?
SILLY ! THIS ISN'T HIS REAL BODY, OF COURSE.
DADDY HAS THE BIGGEST COLLECTION OF SPARE BODIES ON ICE IN ZERO CITY. HE LIKES TO GO OFF AND HAVE ADVENTURES IN THEM.
TONIGHT'S WAS A DOOZY, THANKS TO YOU, TANNER. I'LL CREDIT YOU WITH FIVE HUNDRED FOR YOUR TROUBLE. HOPE THERE'S NO HARD FEELINGS.
THERE'S PLENTY OF HARD FEELINGS, MR VAN PEETERS, AND I'D LIKE TO PUT YOU ACROSS MY KNEE. ONLY THING STOPPING ME IS BRUCE, YOUR ALL-PURPOSE FLYING MINDER. BUT MAKE IT A THOUSAND AND I'LL FORGET ALL ABOUT IT.
SURE THING.
The End

MOON RUNNERS
"THE HOMECOMING"
2000 AD
SCRIPT SYDNEY FALCO
ART MASSIMO BELARDINELLI
LETTERING KID ROBSON
THE SPIRIT OF St LOUIS, A MOONRUNNING FREIGHTER CAPTAINED BY A MAN CALLED FLYNN, PREPARES TO RECEIVE A PRECIOUS CARGO.
TEN SECONDS TO DOCKING, CAPTAIN.
THANK YOU, MR KEMPO. HAVE ALL HANDS STAND BY TO EMBRACE THE BITCH.
NUMBER ONE, WHY ARE YOU AT THE HELMSMAN'S STATION?
I RELIEVED MR GOETHE OF HIS DUTIES, CAPTAIN.
INDEED? IS HE IN SOME WAY INCAPACITATED?
IN A MANNER OF SPEAKING... HE'S UPSET!
"UPSET"?
WHY IS HE UPSET?

"I PUT HIM ON LOOK-OUT DUTY...
"HE CAN STILL SCREEN THE SHIP FROM THE PSYCHIC TURBULENCE OF SUB-SPACE...
"BUT HE'S IN NO FIT STATE TO PILOT THE SHIP..."
"I'M GETTING A LITTLE TIRED OF THIS, KEMPO. I WANT TO KNOW WHAT'S WRONG WITH GOETHE."
"WELL...AH...HE'S HOMESICK, CAPTAIN."
"HOMESICK. IS THIS A JOKE?"
"WELL, NOT HOMESICK. IT'S SOMETHING MORE COMPLEX.
"THE PSYCHICS OF GOETHE'S HOMEWORLD—THE JIANS—ARE A RACE APART, WITH THEIR OWN CUSTOMS AND CULTURE.
"YOUNG JIANS ARE SEPARATED FROM THEIR PARENTS AT AN EARLY AGE...

"...AND REARED IN ISOLATION FOR THE FIRST FEW YEARS.
"DEPRIVED OF CONTACT WITH THEIR OWN KIND AND SUBJECTED TO A BARRAGE OF PSI-ENHANCING EXERCISES, JIANS DEVELOP STAGGERING MENTAL POWERS BY THE TIME THEY'RE TWELVE.
"IN THEIR THIRTEENTH YEAR, WHEN A YOUNG JIAN COMPLETES HIS PSYCHIC TRAINING, THERE IS A BIG PARTY...
"...THEN THEY RETURN TO LIVE AS YOUNG ADULTS IN THE COLLECTIVE CARE OF THE COMMUNITY.
VERY INTERESTING, NUMBER ONE. BUT WHAT HAS ALL THIS TO DO WITH GOETHE GETTING SICK?
I'M COMING TO THAT, CAPTAIN.

AFTER A JIAN IS AWAY FROM HOME A FEW YEARS, HE DEVELOPS A **HOMESICKNESS...**
IT REALLY **IS** A SICKNESS, TOO.
SO UNLESS WE GET GOETHE BACK TO HIS OWN KIND **SOON**, HIS PSI-ABILITIES WILL RUN **OUT OF CONTROL...**
HE'LL LOSE TOUCH WITH THE REAL WORLD...UNTIL HE JUST **LEAVES** IT BEHIND.
HE'LL DIE.
SO, HOW LONG HAVE WE GOT ?
DIFFICULT TO SAY. DAYS. HOURS.
MAYBE HE WON'T LAST LONG ENOUGH TO GET US TO ALTAIR-4 TO DELIVER THESE MED-SUPPLIES TO THE BELLEROPHON EXPEDITION.
HE WON'T **HAVE** TO...
THE SAFETY OF MY SHIP AND CREW COMES FIRST. SET A COURSE FOR GOETHE'S HOMEWORLD !
AYE, AYE, CAP'N.

AND AS THE SPIRIT PLUNGES INTO SUB-SPACE, THE **WEIRDNESS** BEGINS...
I THOUGHT YOU SAID GOETHE WOULD SHIELD US FROM THE WORST OF IT...
HE **IS**, CAP'N.
IS IT JUST ME, OR IS IT GETTING WARM?
I'LL CHECK...
BRIDGE TO COGG...
...STATUS REPORT ON LIFE-SUPPORT SYSTEMS FOR CAP'N FLYNN.
IT'S HOT! **DAMN** HOT!
BUT I DIDN'T KNOW IT WAS **THAT** HOT!
HE SAYS IT'S **HOT**, CAP'N... DAMN—
I **HEARD** WHAT HE SAID, NUMBER ONE.
"EVERYONE'S A FREAKING **COMEDIAN** AROUND HERE."

HOW FAR ARE WE OUT FROM GOETHE'S WORLD, KEMPO?
DIFFICULT TO SAY, CAP'N. THE INSTRUMENTS APPEAR TO BE MELTING.
THE WHOLE BRIDGE IS MELTING...AH, THIS IS JUST AN ILLUSION, ISN'T IT?
I HOPE SO.
CAN'T YOU GET ANY MORE SPEED OUT OF HER, KEMPO?
I'M ROWING AS FAST AS I CAN, CAP'N.
IT'S GOING TO TAKE A WEEK, AT THIS RATE.
"I HOPE NOT. I DON'T THINK I COULD TAKE A WEEK OF THIS!"

IT OCCURS TO ME, NUMBER ONE, THAT WE'D DO A LITTLE BETTER IF WE COULD GET GOETHE TO **HELP** US...
YOU MIGHT HAVE A POINT...
ONE OF US IS GOING TO HAVE TO GET **THROUGH** TO GOETHE...MAKE HIM **UNDERSTAND.**
WHICH OF US DID YOU HAVE IN MIND, SIR?
JUST GET **ON** WITH IT...
AH, GOETHE? CAN YOU HEAR ME?
YES, I HEAR YOU, MOTHER.
WE NEED YOUR HELP, GOETHE. YOU'RE **SICK** AND WE HAVE TO GET YOU **HOME**, BUT WE CAN'T PILOT THE SHIP WITHOUT YOU.
AH, **HOME**, YOU SAY? I THINK I CAN MAKE THE SHIP TAKE US HOME.
JUST LIE BACK, RELAX, CLOSE YOUR EYES AND IN A TRICE...

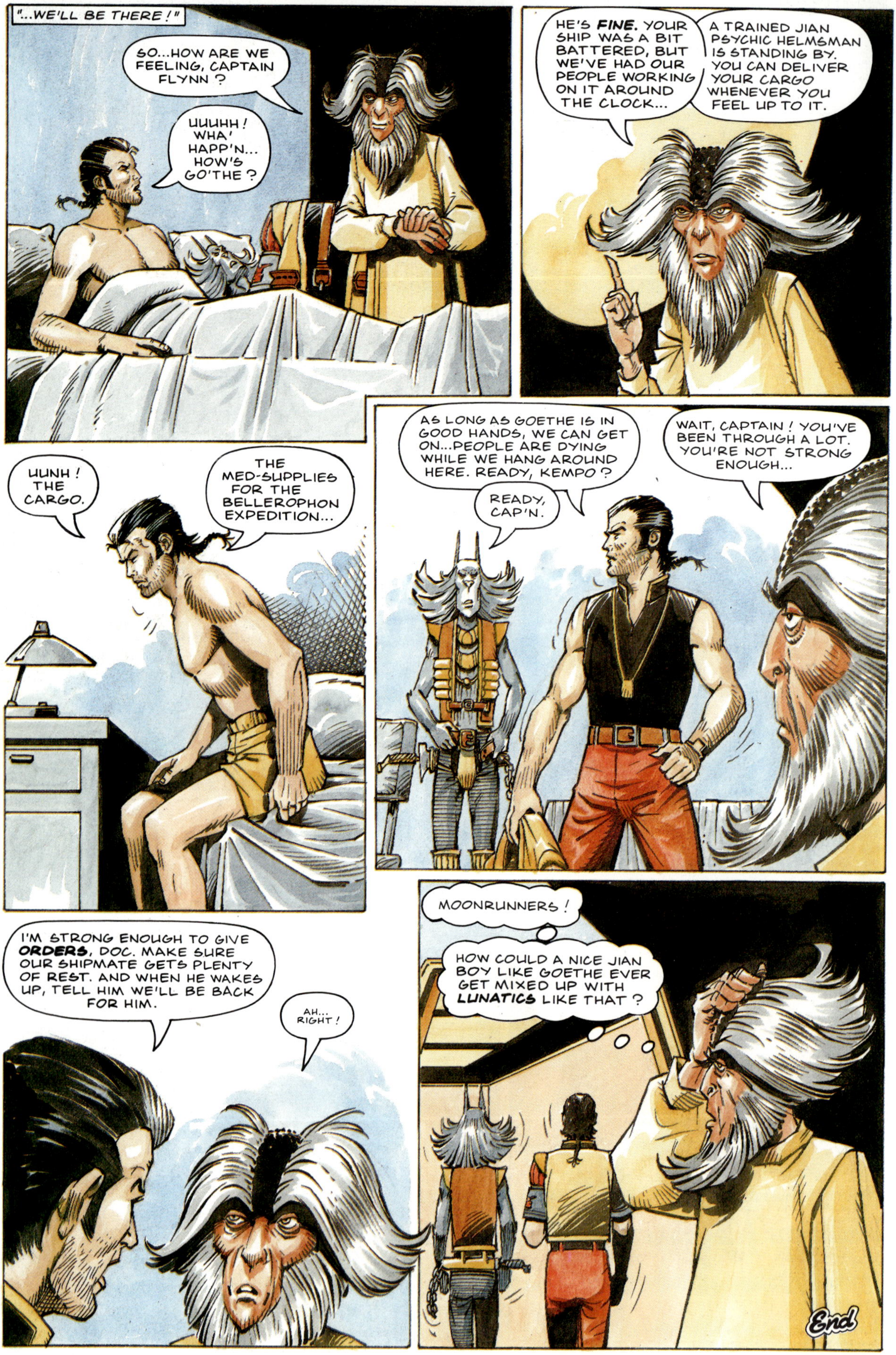
"...WE'LL BE THERE!"
SO...HOW ARE WE FEELING, CAPTAIN FLYNN?
UUUHH! WHA' HAPP'N... HOW'S GO'THE?
HE'S FINE. YOUR SHIP WAS A BIT BATTERED, BUT WE'VE HAD OUR PEOPLE WORKING ON IT AROUND THE CLOCK...
A TRAINED JIAN PSYCHIC HELMSMAN IS STANDING BY. YOU CAN DELIVER YOUR CARGO WHENEVER YOU FEEL UP TO IT.
UUNH! THE CARGO.
THE MED-SUPPLIES FOR THE BELLEROPHON EXPEDITION...
AS LONG AS GOETHE IS IN GOOD HANDS, WE CAN GET ON...PEOPLE ARE DYING WHILE WE HANG AROUND HERE. READY, KEMPO?
READY, CAP'N.
WAIT, CAPTAIN! YOU'VE BEEN THROUGH A LOT. YOU'RE NOT STRONG ENOUGH...
I'M STRONG ENOUGH TO GIVE ORDERS, DOC. MAKE SURE OUR SHIPMATE GETS PLENTY OF REST. AND WHEN HE WAKES UP, TELL HIM WE'LL BE BACK FOR HIM.
AH... RIGHT!
MOONRUNNERS!
HOW COULD A NICE JIAN BOY LIKE GOETHE EVER GET MIXED UP WITH LUNATICS LIKE THAT?
End

DROIDS LIFESTYLE QUESTIONNAIRE

FAVOURITE 2000 AD STORY

Judge Dredd

FAVOURITE FOODS

1. *Chinese*
2. *Italian*
3. *Indian (on the same plate)*

FAVOURITE RECORDS

1. *Kiss – Alive*
2. *Kate Bush – The Whole Story*
3. *Des O'Connor – The Hits*

PREFERRED COMPANY ON DESERT ISLAND

Chinese Chippy

MOST IRRITATING HABIT

Waking up late

FAVOURITE SHOP

The Forbidden Planet

IDEAL NEXT PRIME MINISTER

Dirty Harry

FAVOURITE BIRTHSIGN

Cancer

FAVOURITE COMPUTER GAME

Fiddle The Bank Account

FAVOURITE MOVIES

1. *James Bond*
2. *Laurel and Hardy*
3. *Old Hollywood Horror's*

DESIGNATION *Marshall Art I*

FAVOURITE OFF-DUTY PASTIMES

1. *Staying in bed*
2. *Reading*
3. *Breathing*

LAST BOOK READ

Janet and John Go Shopping

FAVOURITE NEWSPAPER

Weatherfield Recorder

WHY?

It's so hardhitting

FAVOURITE TV SHOW

I, Claudius

FAVOURITE FIGURE IN TERRAN HISTORY

Eddie 'The Eagle' Edwards

IN THE GASBAH QUARTER OF DESERT CITY KYRO, ROGUE TROOPER HAS SURVIVED AN ATTEMPT ON HIS LIFE. THE 'MURDER' WEAPON, HOWEVER, INTERESTS HIM...
IT'S OF NORT ORIGIN. WAS IT PICKED UP BY THE LOCALS, OR COULD IT MEAN SOMETHING MORE SINISTER...
LIKE NORT INFILTRATION OF THE GASBAH?
"BUT WE'RE WELL AWAY FROM THE FRONT LINE HERE. JUST DESERT OUTSIDE THE CITY...
"...AND INSIDE, THE GASBAH IS SECTIONED OFF AND GUARDED BY MILITARY FUZZ. NO-ONE IS SUPPOSED TO GO IN OR OUT."
ALIENS-ONLY ZONE NO HUMANS
BUT SOME DO, TO TRADE WITH OTHER GASBAHS ACROSS THE DESERT. LIKE THAT STAMEL RIDER DOWN THERE WHO'S JUST COME IN.
YEAH, THAT COULD BE HOW THE NORTS GET AGENTS INTO THE GASBAH.
ROGUE DECIDED TO INVESTIGATE HIS SUSPICIONS. IN THE BAR...
BAGMAN, CHECK OUT THE CROWD. SEE IF THAT RIDER IS HERE.
SURE THING, ROGUE. STRONG READING OF STAMEL ODOUR COMING FROM THE LEFT..!
ROGUE TROOPER
THE GASBAH — Part 3
SCRIPT ROBOT GERRY FINLEY-DAY
ART ROBOT CAM KENNEDY
LETTERING ROBOT BILL NUTTALL

BAGMAN'S SENSORS SWIFTLY LOCATED THE RIDER...
STRANGE LOOKING CHARACTER. TRANSLATE FOR ME, BAGMAN.
SYNTH PASTIS
HEY, PAL, BUY YOU A DRINK? AIMING TO MAKE THE DESERT RUN MYSELF TOMORROW. HOW'S THINGS OUT THERE?
HAGAHA AA CHE-CHE-COSSS?
NO REACTION.
I'M GETTING BODY-SCAN READINGS THAT SHOW TALKIN' WON'T HELP, ROGUE...
...'CAUSE HE'S NO ALIEN— HE'S A NORT!
HE KNOWS WE'VE SUSSED HIM!
CAN'T MOVE! HE'S TAKEN THE BUBBLE DANCER HOSTAGE!
HELP! IF HE CUTS MY CHEM-SUIT, I'M FINISHED!
THE GIRL ENTERTAINER— ONE OF THE FEW HUMANS IN THE GASBAH— WAS PROTECTED FROM THE POISON AIR BY A SEALED SUIT.
DAREN'T RISK A DIRECT ASSAULT. MAYBE I CAN SURPRISE HIM WITH GUNNAR...
ROGUE'S LIGHTNING BRAIN CALCULATED ANGLES, VELOCITIES AND...

SIXTY DEGREE ELEVATION, VELOCITY MARK TWO — SINGLE SHOT. . .
NOW!
KLIK
BLAAM
BEEOOW
THE BULLET RICOCHETED OFF THE CEILING, AND. . .
AAAH!
YOU SAVED MY LIFE, G.I. YOU MUST STAY— LET ME SHOW YOU MY GRATITUDE. . .
ROGUE, WE'VE GOT WORK TO DO. . .
THANKS FOR THE OFFER, MA'AM, BUT WE'RE FROM DIFFERENT WORLDS. BEST WE STICK TO THEM.
HMMM — REMOVED ORGANS, REMODELLED SKULL, SKIN GRAFTS. THE NORT GENE-GENIES WENT TO A LOT OF TROUBLE TO PASS THIS NORT OFF AS AN ALIEN!
AND WHAT'S THIS, TUCKED IN HIS CLOTHES?
GENE-GENIE — GENETIC ENGINEER.
A MOUTHPIECE — A NORT MESSAGE POD!

ROGUE ACTIVATED THE POD.
AGENTS OF NORDLAND, WE OF THE GENERAL STAFF SALUTE YOU. YOUR SUICIDE MISSION IN THE GASBAH WILL BE THE KEY TO OUR VICTORY IN THE DESERT ZONE. OUR GLORIOUS ARMY WILL . . .
I WAS RIGHT! A NEST OF NORTS HERE, AMONG THE ALIS – BUT WHAT IS THEIR MISSION?
FIRST, I GOTTA WARN KYRO COMMAND. GET THIS MOUTH-PIECE TO THE MILITARY FUZZ AT THE GASBAH GATES... UH...YEAH, GOTTA...
ROGUE – WHAT'S WRONG?
RIXBAH
DUNNO.. FEEL.. DIZZY. CAN'T BE.. GASBAH AIR.. CAN IT...?
GETTING ..UH... WORSE..
KEEP GOING, ROGUE. CHECKPOINT DEAD AHEAD!
SOMETHIN' ..UH.. WRONG. SOUTHER FUZZ NOT.. MOVING...

OH.. UH.. THEY'RE **DEAD!** PARALYSED BY NORT WEAPONS... WHERE THEY... **STOOD!**
RUN, ROGUE! SENSORS PICKING UP NORT LIFE-FORMS BEHIND US!
YEAH.. RR.. RUN... RR... MUST.. GET THE MESSAGE ... OUT!
BUT...
NORTS... SHOWING THEMSELVES, AND I CAN'T RESIST...
TAKE HIM BACK TO THE GASBAH, AGENTS TEN AND TWELVE.
STAY OUT OF THIS, ALIEN.
XAH! XAH! XISS?
THE NORTS HAD PRODUCED A VIRUS WHICH COULD AFFECT A G.I.'S BLOODSTREAM.
VIRUS X, G.I. THAT WAS WHAT THE RIDER BROUGHT IN TO-NIGHT, JUST TO DEAL WITH YOU.
BUT HOW...?
THROUGH **ME**, TROOPER. MY CHEM-SUIT WAS IMPREGNATED WITH THE TOXIN. WHEN I TOUCHED YOU JUST NOW IT ENTERED THROUGH YOUR SKIN PORES.
THE DANCER!
RIGHT! I'M PART OF THE GASBAH INFILTRATION, AND BEFORE WE PUT OUR PLAN INTO OPERATION **I'LL DANCE ON YOUR GRAVE, G.I.!**

DROIDS LIFESTYLE QUESTIONNAIRE

DESIGNATION *John Smith*

FAVOURITE 2000 AD STORY

Chopper

FAVOURITE FOODS

1. *Mousaka*
2. *Lambs' Kidneys*
3. *Chilli Con Carne*

FAVOURITE RECORDS

1. *Talking Heads – "Speaking In Tongues"*
2. *Brian Eno & David Byrne – "My Life In The Bush of Ghosts"*
3. *Phillip Glass – "The Photographer"*

PREFERRED COMPANY ON DESERT ISLAND

Jonathan Miller

MOST IRRITATING HABIT

*Getting up at 1 o'clock in the afternoon and compulsively sniffing my armpits**

FAVOURITE SHOP

Clone Zone

IDEAL NEXT PRIME MINISTER

Jonathan Miller

FAVOURITE BIRTHSIGN

Leo

FAVOURITE COMPUTER GAME

Lost Caves

FAVOURITE MOVIES

1. *"12 Angry Men"*
2. *"Stalker"*
3. *"The Wicker Man"*

**. . . and occasionally other people's.*

FAVOURITE OFF-DUTY PASTIMES

1. *Talking about myself in a loud voice*
2. *Licking batteries*
3. *Doing impressions of Jonathan Miller*

LAST BOOK READ

If You Could See Me Now – Peter Straub

FAVOURITE NEWSPAPER

None

WHY?

They're all boring

FAVOURITE TV SHOW

"After Dark" & "Hit Man And Her"

FAVOURITE FIGURE IN TERRAN HISTORY

Ray McAnally

COVERS -The Dro

MICK AUSTIN *(Art Droid)*

◀ Prog 613 by Steve Yeowell

Because: "I like the colours and it reminds me of my mother."

NIGEL DOBBYN *(Art Droid)*

Prog 657 by Kev Hopgood ▶

Because: "of its strong linework, clean design and the impact of its monochromatic effect."

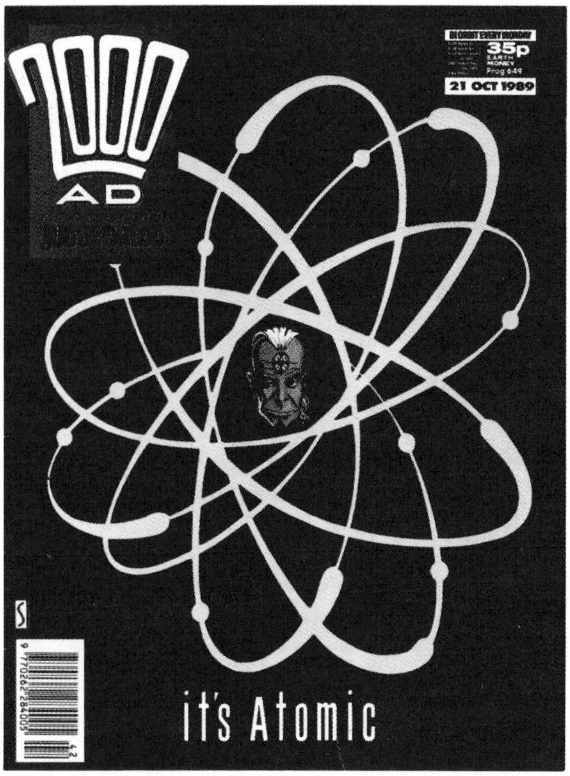

BRETT EWINS *(Art Droid)*

◀ Prog 649 by Steve Cook

Because: "It is an original idea with excellent graphic design. It was full of colour in a reserved and structured manner and thereby creates great impact. The black background throws the whole design into perfect relief, making it a classic cover."

OF 1989
s Decide

This year I would like to pick something by Bisley cos I didn't pick him last year and I know he gets upset about these things.

Simon.

SIMON HARRISON
(Art Droid)
Something by Simon Bisley ▶
Because: "Just because."

ALAN GRANT *(Script Droid)*
◀ Prog 617 by Simon Harrison
Because: "It's nice to see some one do something completely original and not rip off another artist's material."

DUNCAN FEGREDO
(Art Droid)
Prog 626 by Simon Bisley ▶
Because: "It doesn't look like a comic book cover. . . it's more like a poster for a cinemascope movie."

JOHN HIGGINS *(Art Droid)*
Prog 636 by Colin MacNeil ▶
Because: "I've always wanted a pair of furry dice for my car mirror but couldn't find any. Now I have the next best thing hanging from it . . . Prog 636. What Thrill-Power!"

KEV HOPGOOD *(Art Droid)*
◀ Prog 647 by Steve Cook
Because: "It's bright, colourful and I like Elsa Lanchester."

GRAHAM HIGGINS *(Art Droid)*
Prog 658 by Richard Dolan ▶
Because: "It's so clever of Tharg to discover a missing Cistine Chapel panel."

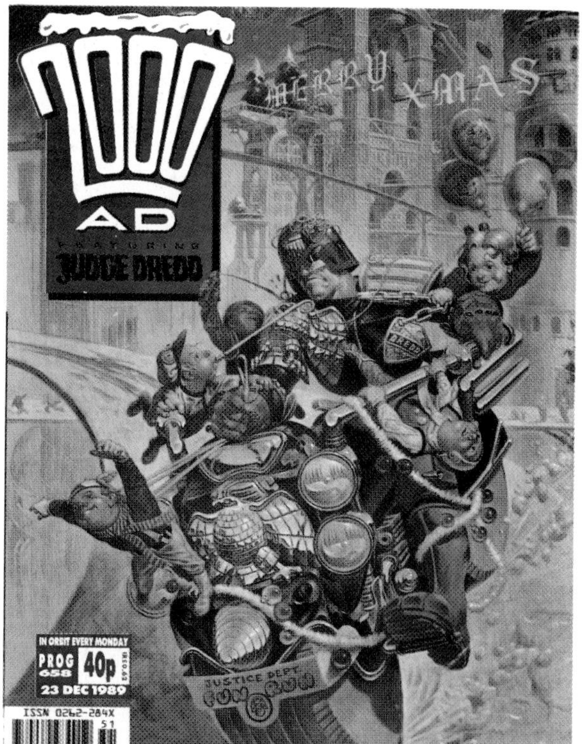

MAC I *(Editorial Droid)*

Prog 650 by John Higgins ▶

Because: “It combines brilliant artwork with a new era of Thrill-Power. Nice one, John – Nice one, Tharg!”

COLIN MacNEIL *(Art Droid)*

◀ Prog 634 by John Higgins

Because: “It's basically a strong, simple design against a non-descript background, with good use of co-ordinated colours and just the right amount of detail in the right places to give the subtle feeling that Dredd's about to step out of the page and whack the reader around the head with that big stick.”

PAUL MARSHALL *(Art Droid)*

◀ Prog 627 by Steve Yeowell

Because: “I like it!”

BRENDAN McCARTHY *(Art Droid)*
Prog 615 by Rian Hughes ▶
Because: "I said so. He's in love with me and I feel fine."

JIM McCARTHY *(Art Droid)*
◀ Prog 649 by Steve Cook
Because: "It's dead simple and simple is best. Nice pic of Tharg and good design with a strong coverline. You look, see, absorb, register. That's comics, folks!"

ALAN McKENZIE *(Script Droid)*
◀ Prog 634 by John Higgins
Because: "John Higgins knows how to put together a cover that grabs the attention."

KID ROBSON *(Lettering Droid)*
Prog 637 by Steve Cook ▶
Because: "The definition of Thrill-Power describes perfectly the effect my dynamic, devastating and devilish good looks have on the female of the species. (Please excuse the crayon, but they don't allow me sharp objects in here!)"

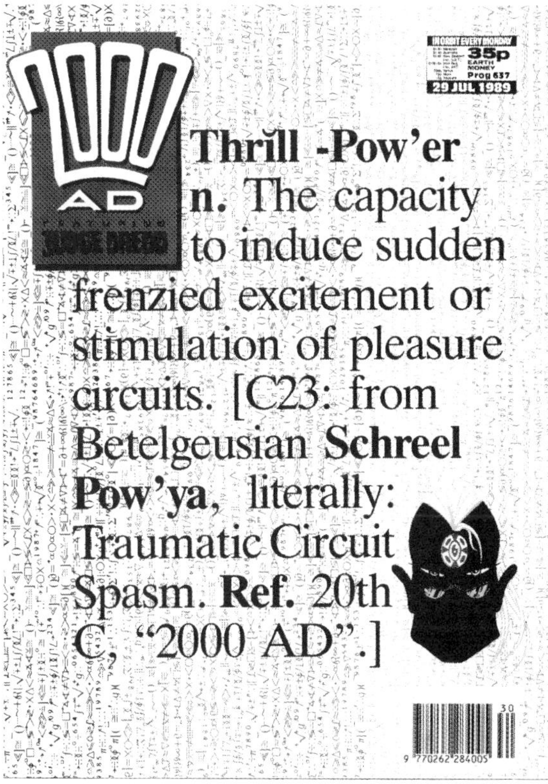

JOHN SMITH *(Script Droid)*
◀ Prog 646 by Sean Phillips
Because: "Judge Dredd reminds me of the man in the Athena poster. I mean, can you imagine him holding a cute little baby on those hands?"

JOHN TOMLINSON *(Script Droid)*
Prog 613 by Steve Yeowell ▶
Because: "The face of Judge Death is a heartwarming reminder that not even advanced decomposition, banishment to limbo and membership of a psychotic inter-dimensional hit squad need present any serious threat to impeccable dental hygiene. And Anderson's nice, too."

ROGUE TROOPER HAS UNCOVERED A NORT INFILTRATION UNIT IN THE GASBAH QUARTER OF KYRO. NOW, DRUGGED WITH VIRUS X, HE IS TAKEN BACK TO THE UNIT'S SECRET BASE...
COME ON IN, BIG BOY. WE'VE CLEARED THE BAR FOR OUR OWN 'PRIVATE' PARTY...
THE BARMAN... SO YOU'RE PART OF THE... INFILTRATION...
COUGH I'M A VET, LIKE I SAID, COUGH A NORT VET. YOU KNOW WE'RE HERE, TROOPER, NOW LOOK IN THE CELLAR AND SEE WHY!
ROGUE TROOPER
THE GASBAH — Part 4
...OX-BOTTLES — THOUSANDS OF THEM
RIGHT, SOUTHER. AND THIS CELLAR RUNS UNDER MOST OF THE GASBAH. IT'S ONE BIG SUPPLY DUMP!

"NOW OUR MAIN DESERT FORCE IS APPROACHING AND IT WILL BE HERE BY DAWN.
WE'VE BEEN USING OUR RE-GENED STAMEL RIDERS TO SMUGGLE THE BOTTLES IN FOR MONTHS. NOBODY SUSPECTED A THING...
"WE WILL BE READY TO RE-SUPPLY THEM WITH AIR FOR THEIR SUITS AND VEHICLES, AND THEN...
"...KYRO WILL FALL TO THE NORTS!"
IT'LL...NEVER ...WORK...
HAH! SOUTHER FOOL! WE HAVE ELIMINATED THE MILITARY FUZZ AT THE ENTRY GATES AND DRUGGED YOU WITH VIRUS X. YOU ARE HELPLESS!
LEAVE HIM, WOMAN. WE HAVE WORK TO DO BELOW, AND OUR GLORIOUS ARMY DRAWS EVER CLOSER!
AND...
WE'RE ON OUR OWN, ROGUE. WISH I COULD BE OF MORE USE TO YOU, LIKE GUNNAR OR BAG-MAN—
N-NOT ALONE, HELM...SOMETHING ON...CEILING...

THATA GOHH SEL?
WHAT THE—?
GOHH GOHEEH?
THEY'RE ALIEN LIFE FORMS! HELM, SEE IF YOU CAN PATCH IN TO BAGMAN... NEED TRANSLATION...
ROGUE'S BIO-CHIPPED BACKPACK HAD BEEN TAKEN BELOW, ALONG WITH GUNNAR. BUT A COM-LINK WAS STILL OPEN...
READ YOU, HELM. RELAY AUDIO, I'LL TRANSLATE.
COMIN' THROUGH. <GOH CEL RTE...>
GOT IT. THEY'RE **RONDONIANS.** SO FAR THEY'VE BEEN UNDETECTED BY THE NORTS BECAUSE THEY LOOK LIKE PART OF THE FUNGUS THAT GROWS IN THE GASBAH.
A-ASK THEM TO HELP...
KROGGA THPEE TR SOLLT...
THEY SAY THAT THEY'RE **PACIFISTS.** THEY DON'T WANT ANY TROUBLE THAT MIGHT DRAW ATTENTION TO THEM. THE GASBAH IS THE ONLY HOME THEY'VE GOT SINCE THEIR ANCESTORS' WORLD WAS DESTROYED.
DON'T THINK THEY'RE GOING TO BE MUCH HELP, ROGUE.
W-WAIT... DID YOU SAY THEY'RE NATIVES OF.. **RONDO?** THAT WAS A **NEUTRAL** PLANET, D-DESTROYED LONG TIME AGO, EARLY DAYS OF WAR, BY... BY...
BY THE NORTS! THAT'S RIGHT, ROGUE. ONE OF THEIR EARLIEST CONQUESTS. BET THESE RONDONIANS DIDN'T REALISE THAT!

TOO RIGHT! PICKING UP A BABBLE OF VOICES. SHOCK. SURPRISE. ANGER. I THINK THEY'RE CHANGIN' THEIR MINDS...
LOOKS LIKE WE'VE GOT SOME ALLIES!
GERR ONNI MO!
HE'S COMING OVER TO SEE IF WE CAN BE HELPED, ROGUE!
GREEHS KREK CHO LDD!
TRANSLATION COMING THROUGH. HE SAYS THAT HE'S...
STOOSH
GRAAAEEEEEEE!
WELL, WELL. LOOKS AS THOUGH I DIDN'T KNOW ALL THE 'REGULARS' IN MY BAR.
THOSE THINGS ARE A THREAT! GET RID OF THEM!
PTTOWW!
PTTOW!
LEAVE NO SURVIVORS!
PTTOW!

H-HGR!! TLSS..SS.. GR..
ONE ON THE G.I. PACK!
THIS ICE-BREAKER WILL FINISH IT!
AND...
THAT'S ALL OF 'EM ACCOUNTED FOR. TOO BAD, G.I.
BUT ROGUE SPOTTED SOMETHING CONCEALED IN THE ALIEN FORM...
SEAL BURSTER BOMB! BAGMAN MUST HAVE SLIPPED IT TO THE ALI!
I CAN EXPLODE THIS AMONGST THOSE OX-BOTTLES — BLOW THE NORTS' INVASION SKY-HIGH!
BUT SOMEHOW I'VE GOT TO WARN THE ALIENS AND THE WHOLE OF KYRO TO TAKE COVER FIRST — WITHOUT ALERTING THE NORTS!
2000 A.D. Credit Card:
SCRIPT ROBOT GERRY FINLEY-DAY
ART ROBOT CAM KENNEDY
LETTERING ROBOT BILL NUTTALL
COMPU-73E

Fiends of the Eastern Front

Flesh

continued from page 34

Mach-0

Title: Mach-0 Book 1.
Progs 65-75.
From 20/05/78 to 29/07/78.
11 Eps. 55 pages.
Script: Steve MacManus.
Art: Sola.

Title: Mach-0 Book 2.
Progs 162-165.
From 26/04/80 to 14/06/80.
4 Eps. 18 pages.
Script: Ian Rogan (Steve MacManus).
Art: Mike Dorey.

Mach-1

Title: Mach-1 Book 1.
Progs 1-46.
From 26/02/77 to 07/01/78.
46 Eps. 263 pages.
Script: Mills/Preston/Wagner/MacManus.
Art: Enio/Cooper/Redondo/Dorey.

Title: Mach-1 Book 2.
Progs 53-64.
From 25/02/78 to 13/05/78.
12 Eps. 59 pages.
Script: MacManus/Mills.
Art: Redondo/Montero.

Mean Arena

Title: Mean Arena Book 1.
Progs 178-202.
From 20/09/80 to 07/03/81.
19 Eps. 76 pages.
Script: Tom Tully.
Art: John Richardson.

Title: Mean Arena Book 2.
Progs 218-282.
From 27/06/81 to 18/09/82.
53 Eps. 205 pages.
Script: Tom Tully.
Art: Dillon/Bradbury/White.

Mean Team

Title: Mean Team.
Progs 437-447.
From 28/09/85 to 07/12/85.
Eps. 53 pages.
Script: Alan Grant.
Art: Massimo Belardinelli.

Title: Return of the Mean Team.
Progs 525-541.
From 06/06/87 to 26/09/87.
14 Eps. 60 pages.
Script: Alan Hebden.
Art: Massimo Belardinelli.

Title: Survivor.
Progs 639-644.
From 12/08/89 to 16/09/89.
6 Eps. 30 pages.
Script: Hilary Robinson.
Art: Ron Smith.

Medivac 318

Title: Medivac 318.
Progs 619-640.
From 25/03/89 to 19/08/89.
12 Eps. 72 pages.
Script: Hilary Robinson.
Art: Nigel Dobbyn.

Meltdown Man, The

Title: Meltdown Man, The.
Progs 178-227.
From 20/09/80 to 29/08/81.
50 Eps. 120 pages.
Script: Alan Hebden.
Art: Massimo Belardinelli.

Metalzoic

Title: Metalzoic.
Progs 483-492.
From 16/08/86 to 18/10/86.
10 Eps. 64 pages.
Script: Pat Mills.
Art: Kev O'Neill.

Mind of Wolfie Smith, The

Title: Mind of Wolfie Smith, The Book 1.
Progs 127-145.
From 25/08/79 to 29/12/79.
18 Eps. 68 pages.
Script: Tom Tully.
Art: Ian Gibson/Vanyo.

Title: Mind of Wolfie Smith, The Book 2.
Progs 162-177.
From 26/04/80 to 13/09/80.
13 Eps. 62 pages.
Script: Tom Tully.
Art: Redondo.

Moonrunners

Title: Moonrunners.
Progs 591-606.
From 10/09/88 to 24/12/88.
15 Eps. 77 pages.
Script: Parkhouse/McKenzie.
Art: Massimo Belardinelli.

Title: Old Acquaintance.
Progs 641-644.
From 26/08/89 to 16/09/89.
4 Eps. 22 pages.
Script: Alan McKenzie.
Art: Massimo Belardinelli.

Nemesis the Warlock

Title: Terror Tube, The.
Progs 167.
From 05/07/80.
1 Eps. 6 pages.
Script: Pat Mills.
Art: Kev O'Neill.
Reprinted: Best of 2000 AD Monthly 3.

Halo Jones

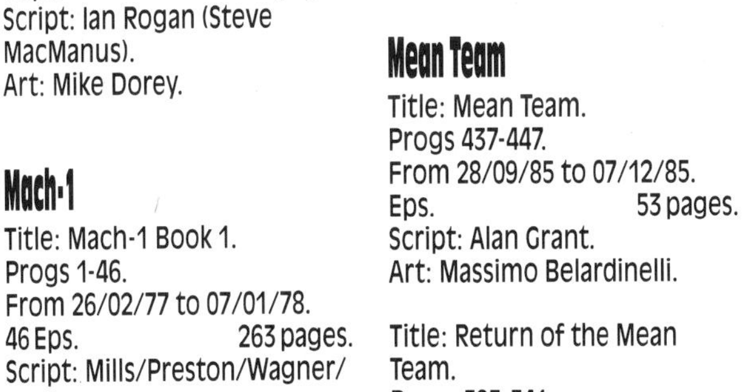

Harlem Heroes

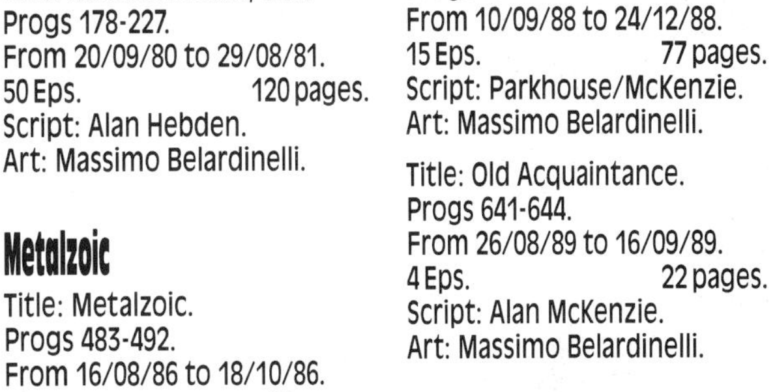

Invasion

Title: Killer Watts.
Progs 178-179.
From 20/09/80 to 27/09/80.
2 Eps. 7 pages.
Script: Pat Mills.
Art: Kev O'Neill.
Reprinted: Best of 2000 AD Monthly 3.

Title: The World of Termight (Book 1).
Progs 222-244.
From 25/07/81 to 26/12/81.
17 Eps. 71 pages.
Script: Pat Mills.
Art: Kev O'Neill.
Reprinted: Best of 2000 AD Monthly 5, 6, 7, 8.

Title: The Alien Alliance (Book 2).
Progs 246-257.
From 09/01/82 to 27/03/82.
12 Eps. 51 pages.
Script: Pat Mills.
Art: Jesus Redondo.
Reprinted: Best of 2000 AD Monthly 43.

Title: The World of Nemesis (Book 3).
Progs 335-348.
From 24/09/83 to 31/12/83.
14 Eps. 67 pages.
Script: Pat Mills.
Art: Kev O'Neill.
Reprinted: Best of 2000 AD Monthly 44.

Title: The Gothic Empire (Book 4).
Progs 387-406.
From 13/10/84 to 25/02/85.
20 Eps. 94 pages.
Script: Pat Mills.
Art: O'Neill/Talbot.
Reprinted: Best of 2000 AD Monthly 38/39.

Title: Ego Trip.
Progs 430.
From 10/08/85.
1 Eps. 6 pages.
Script: Pat Mills.
Art: Kev O'Neill.

Title: Vengeance of Thoth (Book 5).
Progs 435-445.
From 14/09/85 to 23/11/85.
11 Eps. 63 pages.
Script: Pat Mills.
Art: Bryan Talbot.
Reprinted: Best of 2000 AD Monthly 48.

Title: Torquemurder (Book 6).
Progs 482-504.
From 09/08/86 to 10/01/87.
Eps. 59 pages.
Script: Pat Mills.
Art: Bryan Talbot.

Title: Torquemada the God.
Progs 520-524.
From 02/05/87 to 30/05/87.
5 Eps. 25 pages.
Script: Pat Mills.
Art: Kev O'Neill.

Title: Nemesis the Warlock.
Progs 534.
From 08/08/87.
1 Eps. 6 pages.
Script: Pat Mills.
Art: Tony Luke (photographer).

Title: Two Torquemadas, The (Book 7).
Progs 546-557.
From 31/10/87 to 16/01/88.
12 Eps. 61 pages.
Script: Pat Mills.
Art: John Hicklenton.

Title: Purity's Story (Book 8).
Progs 558-566.
From 23/01/88 to.
9 Eps. 45 pages.
Script: Pat Mills.
Art: David Roach.

Title: Deathbringer (Book 9).
Progs 586-608.
From 06/08/88 to 07/01/89.
12 Eps. 61 pages.
Script: Pat Mills.
Art: John Hicklenton.

Night Zero

Title: Night Zero.
Progs 607-616.
From 31/12/88 to 04/03/89.
10 Eps. 51 pages.
Script: John Brosnan.
Art: Kev Hopgood.

Project Overkill

Title: Project Overkill.
Progs 119-126.
From 30/06/79 to 18/08/79.
8 Eps. 32 pages.
Script: Kelvin Gosnell.
Art: Gibson/Redondo.

Return to Armageddon

Title: Return to Armageddon.
Progs 185-218.
From 08/09/80 to 27/06/81.
34 Eps. 137 pages.
Script: Malcolm Shaw.
Art: Jesus Redondo.

Rick Random

Title: Riddle of the Astral Assassin.
Progs 113-118.
From 19/05/79 to 23/06/79.
6 Eps. 33 pages.
Script: Steve Moore.
Art: Ron Turner.

Ro-Busters

Title: Death on the Orient Express.
Progs 86-87.
From 14/10/78 to 21/10/78.
2 Eps. 12 pages.

Mach-1

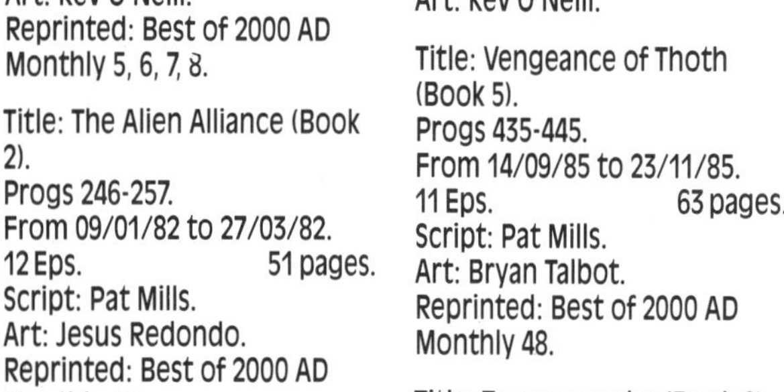

Mean Team

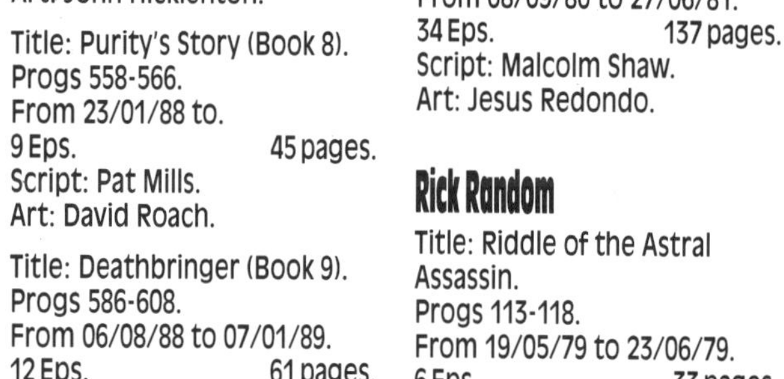

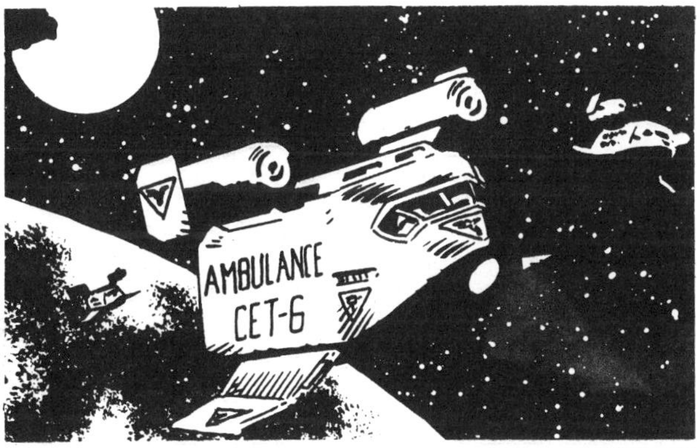

Medivac 318

Metalzoic

Script: Pat Mills.
Art: Dave Gibbons.

Title: Hammerstein's War Memoirs.
Progs 88-92.
From 28/10/78 to 25/11/78.
5 Eps. 30 pages.
Script: Pat Mills.
Art: Dorey/O'Neill/Gibbon/White.
2000 AD Annual 1988.

Title: Ro-Jaws Memoirs.
Progs 93-97.
From 30/12/78 to 27/01/79.
5 Eps. 30 pages.
Script: Pat Mills.
Art: Mike Dorey.

Title: The Terra-Meks.
Progs 98-101.
From 03/02/79 to 24/02/79.
4 Eps. 27 pages.
Script: Pat Mills.
Art: Dave Gibbons.
2000 AD Annual 87.

Title: Fall & Rise of Ro-Jaws and Hammerstein.
Progs 103-115.
From 10/03/79 to 02/06/79.
13 Eps. 78 pages.
Script: Pat Mills.
Art: O'Neill McMahon Dorey.

Robo-Hunter

Title: Verdus.
Progs 76-112.
From 05/08/78 to 12/05/79.
22 Eps. 127 pages.
Script: John Wagner.
Art: Gibson Ferrer.
Reprinted: Best of 2000 AD 51-52.

Title: Day of the Droids.
Progs 152-174.
From 16/02/80 to 23/08/80.
23 Eps. 113 pages.
Script: John Wagner.
Art: Ian Gibson.

Title: Beast of Blackheart Manor.
Progs 259-265.
From 10/04/82 to 22/05/82.
7 Eps. 39 pages.
Script: Alan Grant.
Art: Ian Gibson.
Reprinted: Best of 2000 AD 9.

Title: Filby Case, The.
Progs 266-282.
From 29/05/82 to 10/07/82.
7 Eps. 35 pages.
Script: Alan Grant.
Art: Ian Gibson.
Reprinted: Best of 2000 AD 11.

Title: Killing of Kidd.
Progs 275-281.
From 31/07/82 to 11/09/82.
7 Eps. 35 pages.
Script: Alan Grant.
Art: Ian Gibson.
Reprinted: Best of 2000 AD 12.

Title: Football Crazy.
Progs 283-288.
From 25/09/82 to 30/10/82.
6 Eps. 30 pages.
Script: Wagner/Grant.
Art: Ian Gibson.
Reprinted: Best of 2000 AD 10.

Title: Play It Again, Sam.
Progs 292-307.
From 27/11/82 to 12/03/83.
16 Eps. 82 pages.
Script: Wagner/Grant.
Art: Ian Gibson.

Title: Slaying of Slade.
Progs 312-330.
From 16/04/83 to 20/08/83.
19 Eps. 96 pages.
Script: Wagner/Grant.
Art: Ian Gibson.

Title: Sam Slade's Last Case.
Progs 331-334.
From 27/08/83 to 17/09/83.
4 Eps. 20 pages.
Script: Wagner/Grant.
Art: Ian Gibson.
Reprinted: Best of 2000 AD 26.

Rogue Trooper

Title: Rogue Trooper.
Progs 228-232.
From 05/09/81 to 03/10/81.
31 Eps. 25 pages.
Script: Gerry Finlay-Day.
Art: Dave Gibbons.

Title: Rogue Trooper (2).
Progs 234-241.
From 17/10/89 to 07/12/81.
8 Eps. pages.
Script: Gerry Finlay-Day.
Art: Gibbons/Wilson.

Title: Rogue Trooper (3).
Progs 242-258.
From 12/12/81 to 03/04/82.
15 Eps. 60 pages.
Script: Gerry Finlay-Day.
Art: Dorey/Wilson.

Title: Bagman Blues.
Progs 260-262.
From 17/04/82 to 24/04/82.
3 Eps. 14 pages.
Script: Gerry Finlay-Day.
Art: Brett Ewins.
Reprinted: Best of 2000 AD 7.

Title: The Body Looters.
Progs 265-265.
From 22/05/82 to 22/05/82.
1 Eps. 5 pages.
Script: Gerry Finlay-Day.
Art: Cam Kennedy.
Reprinted: Best of 2000 AD 29.

Title: All Hell on the Dix-I Front.
Progs 266-277.
From 29/05/82 to 14/08/82.
12 Eps. 47 pages.
Script: Gerry Finlay-Day.
Art: Wilson/Kennedy/Ewins.
Reprinted: Best of 2000AD 29.

Title: Assassination Run.
Progs 278-279.

The Mind of Wolfie Smith

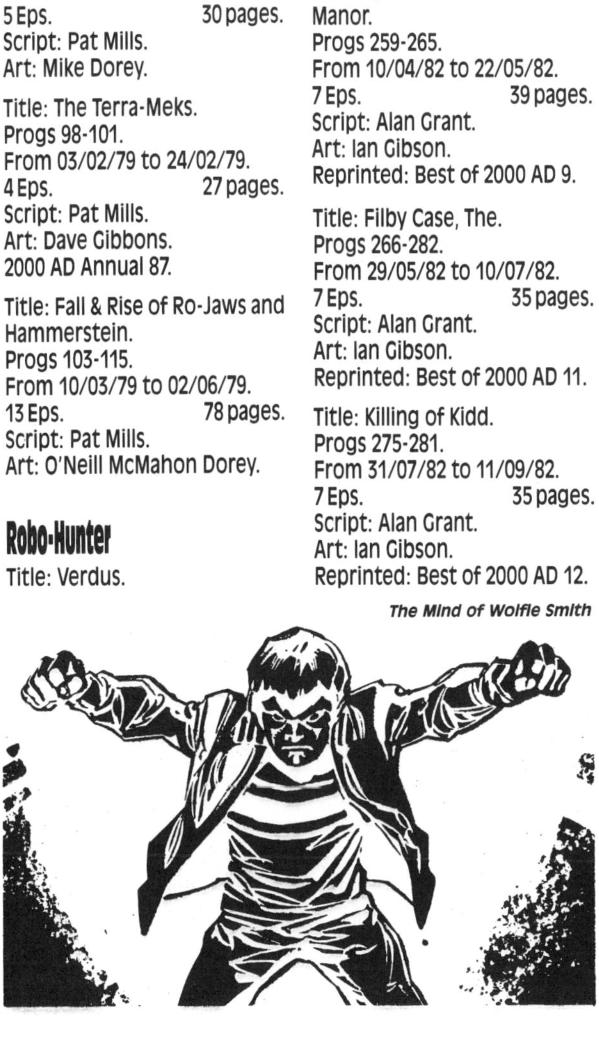

Moonrunners

Nemesis the Warlock

Night Zero

From 21/08/82 to 28/08/82.
2 Eps. 9 pages.
Script: Gerry Finlay-Day.
Art: Cam Kennedy.
Reprinted: Best of 2000 AD 29.

Title: Hats Off to Helm.
Progs 280-281.
From 04/09/82 to 11/09/82.
2 Eps. 8 pages.
Script: Gerry Finlay-Day.
Art: Cam Kennedy.
Reprinted: Best of 2000 AD 45.

Title: Marauders.
Progs 282-289.
From 18/09/82 to 06/11/82.
8 Eps. 35 pages.
Script: Gerry Finlay-Day.
Art: Wilson/Kennedy.

Title: Fort Neuro.
Progs 290-310.
From 20/11/82 to 02/04/82.
19 Eps. 83 pages.
Script: Gerry Finlay-Day.
Art: Ewins/Kennedy.

Title: Major Magnum.
Progs 311-315.
From 09/04/83 to 07/05/83.
5 Eps. 20 pages.
Script: Gerry Finlay-Day.
Art: Brett Ewins.
Reprinted: Best of 2000 AD 8.

Title: Bigfoot.
Progs 316-316.
From 14/05/83 to 14/05/83.
1 Eps. 4 pages.
Script: Gerry Finlay-Day.
Art: Cam Kennedy.

Title: Bio-Wire.
Progs 317-317.
From 21/05/83 to 21/05/83.
1 Eps. 5 pages.
Script: Gerry Finlay-Day.
Art: Cam Kennedy.
Reprinted: Best of 2000 AD 45.

Title: Mill-Com Memories.
Progs 318-322.
From 28/05/83 to 25/06/83.
5 Eps. 22 pages.
Script: Gerry Finlay-Day.
Art: Cam Kennedy.
Reprinted: Best of 2000 AD 10.

Title: Vid-Vultures.
Progs 323-326.
From 02/07/83 to 23/07/83.
4 Eps. 16 pages.
Script: Gerry Finlay-Day.
Art: Brett Ewins.
Reprinted: Best of 2000 AD 45.

Title: Eye of the Traitor.
Progs 327-332.
From 30/07/83 to 03/09/83.
6 Eps. 32 pages.
Script: Gerry Finlay-Day.
Art: Cam Kennedy.
Reprinted: Best of 2000 AD 23.

Title: Frisco Phog.
Progs 333-334.
From 10/09/83 to 17/09/83.
2 Eps. 8 pages.
Script: Gerry Finlay-Day.
Art: Boluda

Title: From Hell to Eternity.
Progs 335-340.
From 24/09/83 to 29/10/83.
6 Eps. 28 pages.
Script: Gerry Finlay-Day.
Art: Brett Ewins
Reprinted: Best of 2000 AD 25.

Title: Mega-Minefield.
Progs 341-342.
From 05/11/83 to 12/11/83.
2 Eps. 10 pages.
Script: Gerry Finlay-Day.
Art: Boluda.

Title: Gasbah.
Progs 343-347.
From 19/11/83 to 11/12/83.
5 Eps. 25 pages.
Script: Gerry Finlay-Day.
Art: Cam Kennedy.
Reprinted: 2000 AD Annual 1991.

Title: Timeslip.
Progs 348-349.
From 24/12/83 to 31/12/83.
2 Eps. 10 pages.
Script: Gerry Finlay-Day.
Art: Boluda.

Title: Colonel Kovert.
Progs 350-355.
From 07/01/84 to 11/02/84.
6 Eps. 24 pages.
Script: Gerry Finlay-Day.
Art: Cam Kennedy.

Title: You Only Die Twice.
Progs 358-368.
From 03/03/84 to 12/05/84.
10 Eps. 42 pages.
Script: Gerry Finlay-Day.
Art: Cam Kennedy.

Title: Message from Milli-Com.
Progs 369-377.
From 19/05/84 to 04/08/84.
9 Eps. 38 pages.
Script: Gerry Finlay-Day.
Art: Cam Kennedy.

Title: Just Routine.
Progs 378-378.
From 11/08/84 to 11/08/84.
1 Eps. 5 pages.
Script: Gerry Finlay-Day.
Art: Trev Goring.

Title: Blind Terror.
Progs 379-380.
From 18/08/84 to 25/08/84.
2 Eps. 10 pages.
Script: Gerry Finlay-Day.
Art: Steve Dillon.

Title: Death Valley.
Progs 381-383.
From 01/09/84 to 15/09/84.
3 Eps. 12 pages.
Script: Gerry Finlay-Day.
Art: Cam Kennedy.

Title: M For Murder.
Progs 384-386.

Rick Random

Ro-Busters

Robo-Hunter

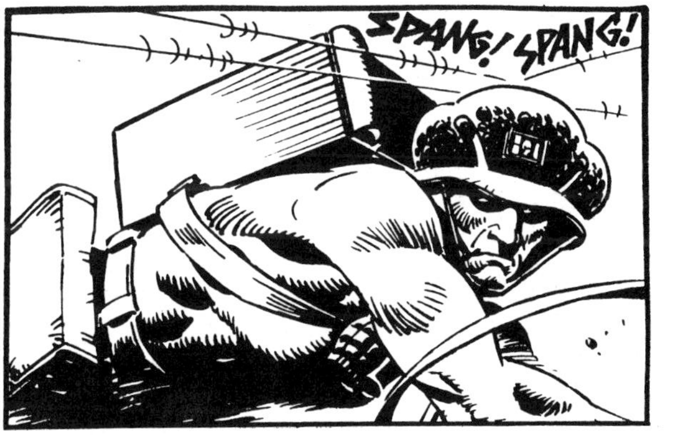

Rogue Trooper

From 22/09/84 to 06/10/84.
3 Eps. 12 pages.
Script: Gerry Finlay-Day.
Art: Cam Kennedy.

Title: To the Ends of Nu Earth.
Progs 387-392.
From 13/10/84 to 17/11/84.
6 Eps. 23 pages.
Script: Gerry Finlay-Day.
Art: Cam Kennedy.

Title: Re-Gene.
Progs 401-406.
From 19/01/85 to 23/02/85.
6 Eps. 36 pages.
Script: Gerry Finlay-Day.
Art: Cam Kennedy.

Title: Return of Rogue Trooper.
Progs 410-419.
From 23/03/85 to 25/05/85.
10 Eps. 40 pages.
Script: Gerry Finlay-Day.
Art: Jose Ortiz.

Title: Antigen of Horst.
Progs 422-432.
From 15/06/85 to 24/08/85.
11 Eps. 45 pages.
Script: Gerry Finlay-Day.
Art: Jose Ortiz.

Title: Return to Milli-Com.
Progs 444-449.
From 16/11/85 to 21/12/85.
6 Eps. 30 pages.
Script: Gerry Finlay-Day.
Art: Jose Ortiz.

Title: The Hit Man.
Progs 495-499.
From 08/11/86 to 06/12/86.
5 Eps. 27 pages.
Script: Geller/MacManus.
Art: Steve Dillon.

Title: Hit One.
Progs 520-531.
From 02/05/87 to 25/07/87.
12 Eps. 61 pages.
Script: Simon Geller.
Art: Steve Dillon.

Title: Hit 2.
Progs 568-572.
From 02/04/88 to 30/04/88.
5 Eps. 27 pages.
Script: Simon Geller.
Art: Steve Dillon.

Title: Hit 3.
Progs 574-575.
From 14/05/88 to 21/05/88.
2 Eps. 12 pages.
Script: Simon Geller.
Art: Steve Dillon.

Title: Hit 4.
Progs 598-603.
From 29/10/88 to 03/12/88.
5 Eps. 32 pages.
Script: Simon Geller.
Art: Steve Dillon.

Title: Nu Earth Flashback.
Progs 624-635.
From 29/04/89 to 15/07/89.
10 Eps. 52 pages.
Script: John Smith.
Art: Dillon/Walker.

Shako

Title: Shako.
Progs 20-35.
From 09/07/77 to 15/10/77.
16 Eps. 76 pages.
Script: Mills/Wagner.
Art: Arancio/Sola/Lopex-Vera.
Reprinted: 2000 AD Annual 1986.

Skizz

Title: Skizz.
Progs 308-330.
From 19/03/83 to 20/08/83.
21 Eps. 94 pages.
Script: Alan Moore.
Art: Jim Baikie.

Sláine

Title: Time Monster, The.
Progs 330.
From 20/08/83.
1 Eps. 6 pages.
Script: Pat Mills.
Art: Massimo Belardinelli.
Reprinted: Best of 2000 AD Monthly 19.

Title: Beast in the Broch, The.
Progs 331-334.
From 27/08/83 to 17/09/83.
4 Eps. 25 pages.
Script: Pat Mills.
Art: Massimo Belardinelli.
Reprinted: Best of 2000 AD Monthly 19.

Title: Warrior's Dawn.
Progs 335.
From 24/09/83.
1 Eps. 6 pages.
Script: Pat Mills.
Art: Mike McMahon.
Reprinted: Best of 2000 AD Monthly 20.

Title: Beltain Giant, The.
Progs 336.
From 01/10/83.
1 Eps. 6 pages.
Script: Pat Mills.
Art: Mike McMahon.
Reprinted: Best of 2000 AD Monthly 20.

Title: Bride of Crom.
Progs 337-342.
From 08/10/83 to 12/11/83.
6 Eps. 36 pages.
Script: Pat Mills.
Art: Massimo Belardinelli.
Reprinted: Best of 2000 AD Monthly 20.

Title: Creeping Death, The.
Progs 343.
From 19/11/83.
1 Eps. 6 pages.
Script: Pat Mills.
Art: Massimo Belardinelli.

Shako
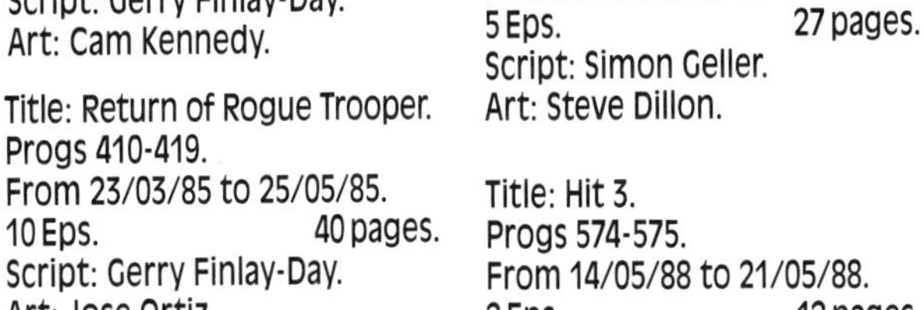

Skizz
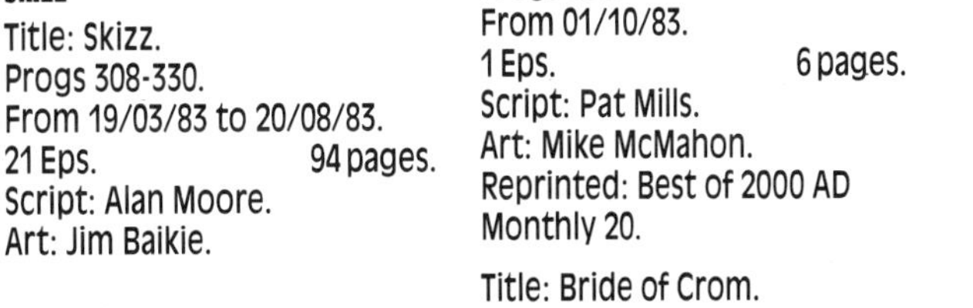

Sláine

Sooner or Later

Title: Bull Dance, The.
Progs 344.
From 26/11/83.
1 Eps. 6 pages.
Script: Pat Mills.
Art: Massimo Belardinelli.

Title: Heroes' Blood.
Progs 345-347.
From 03/12/83 to 17/12/83.
3 Eps. 18 pages.
Script: Pat Mills.
Art: Mike McMahon.

Title: Shoggey Beast, The.
Progs 348-351.
From 24/12/83 to 14/01/84.
4 Eps. 23 pages.
Script: Pat Mills.
Art: Mike McMahon.

Title: Sky Chariots.
Progs 352-360.
From 21/01/84 to 17/03/84.
9 Eps. 52 pages.
Script: Pat Mills.
Art: Mike McMahon.
Reprinted: Best of 2000 AD Monthly 21.

Title: Dragonheist.
Progs 361-367.
From 27/03/84 to 05/05/84.
7 Eps. 49 pages.
Script: Pat Mills.
Art: Massimo Belardinelli.
Reprinted: Best of 2000 AD Monthly 22.

Title: Time Killer, The.
Progs 411-434.
From 30/03/85 to 07/09/85.
22 Eps. 121 pages.
Script: Pat Mills.
Art: Glenn Fabry/David Pugh.
Reprinted: Best of 2000 AD Monthly 33/34.

Title: Tomb of Terror, The.
Progs 447-461.
From 07/12/85 to 15/03/86.
15 Eps. 90 pages.
Script: Pat Mills.
Art: Fabry/Pugh.
Reprinted: Best of 2000 AD Monthly 36/37.

Title: Spoils of Annwn.
Progs 493-499.
From 25/10/86 to 06/12/86.
7 Eps. 43 pages.
Script: Pat Mills.
Art: Collins/Farmer.

Title: Sláine the King.
Progs 500-519.
From 13/12/86 to 25/04/87.
12 Eps. 62 pages.
Script: Pat Mills.
Art: Glenn Fabry.

Title: Sláine the Mini-Series.
Progs 589-591.
From 27/08/88 to 10/09/88.
3 Eps. 14 pages.
Script: Pat Mills.
Art: Glenn Fabry.

Title: Sláine the Horned God Book 1.
Progs 626-635.
From 13/05/89 to 15/07/89.
10 Eps. 60 pages.
Script: Pat Mills.
Art: Simon Bisley.

Sooner or Later

Title: Sooner or Later.
Progs 468-499.
From 03/05/86 to 06/12/86.
32 Eps. 39 pages.
Script: Pete Milligan
Art: Brendan McCarthy.

Title: Swifty's Return.
Progs 614-617.
From 18/02/89 to 11/03/89.
4 Eps. 16 pages.
Script: Pete Milligan
Art: Jamie Hewlett.

Stainless Steel Rat

Title: Stainless Steel Rat.
Progs 140-151.
From 24/11/79 to 09/02/80.
12 Eps. 70 pages.
Script: Kelvin Gosnell.
Art: Carlos Ezquerra.

Title: Stainless Steel Rat Saves the World.
Progs 166-177.
From 21/06/80 to 13/09/80.
12 Eps. 60 pages.
Script: Kelvin Gosnell.
Art: Carlos Ezquerra.

Title: Stainless Steel Rat for President.
Progs 393-404.
From 24/11/84 to 09/02/85.
12 Eps. 62 pages.
Script: Kelvin Gosnell.
Art: Carlos Ezquerra.

Strontium Dog

Title: Strontium Dog.
Progs 86-86.
From 14/10/78 to 14/10/78.
1 Eps. 5 pages.
Script: John Wagner.
Art: Carlos Ezquerra.

Title: Wolrogs, The.
Progs 87-94.
From 21/10/78 t0 06/01/79.
8 Eps. 41 pages.
Script: John Wagner.
Art: Carlos Ezquerra.

Title: Journey into Hell.
Progs 104-118.
From 17/03/79 t0 23/06/79.
15 Eps. 73 pages.
Script: John Wagner.
Art: Carlos Ezquerra.

Title: Death's Head.
Progs 178-181.
From 20/09/80 t0 11/10/80.
4 Eps. 21 pages.

Stainless Steel Rat

Strontium Dog

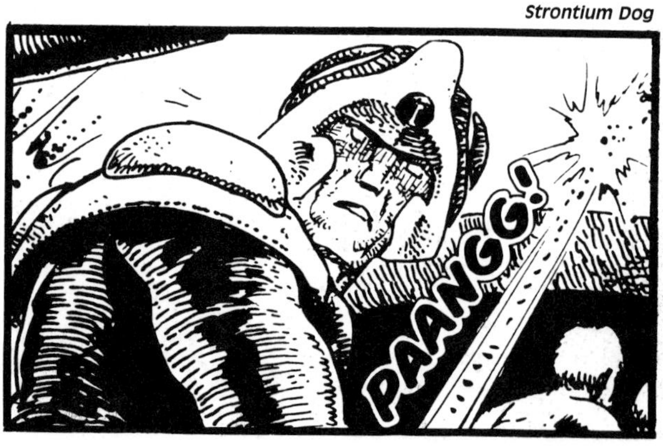

Timequake

Tribal Memories.

Script: Alan Grant.
Art: Carlos Ezquerra.

Title: Schiklegruber Grab, The.
Progs 182-188.
From 18/10/80 to 29/11/80.
7 Eps. 36 pages.
Script: Alan Grant.
Art: Carlos Ezquerra.

Title: Mutie's Luck.
Progs 189.
From 06/12/80.
1 Eps. 6 pages.
Script: Alan Grant.
Art: Carlos Ezquerra.

Title: Doc Quince Case, The.
Progs 190-193.
From 13/12/80 to 03/01/81.
4 Eps. 21 pages.
Script: Alan Grant.
Art: Carlos Ezquerra.

Title: Bad Boys Bust, The.
Progs 194-197.
From 10/01/81 to 31/01/81.
4 Eps. 21 pages.
Script: Alan Grant.
Art: Carlos Ezquerra.

Title: Portrait of a Mutant.
Progs 200-221.
From 21/02/81 to 04/04/81.
19 Eps. 93 pages.
Script: Alan Grant.
Art: Carlos Ezquerra.

Title: Killing, The.
Progs 350-359.
From 07/01/84 to 10/03/84.
10 Eps. 51 pages.
Script: Alan Grant.
Art: Carlos Ezquerra.

Title: Outlaw.
Progs 363-385.
From 07/04/84 to 29/09/84.
23 Eps. 117 pages.
Script: Alan Grant.
Art: Carlos Ezquerra.

Title: Big Bust of 49.
Progs 416-424.
From 04/05/85 to 29/06/85.
9 Eps. 46 pages.
Script: Alan Grant.
Art: Carlos Ezquerra.

Title: Slavers of Drule.
Progs 425-436.
From 06/07/85 to 21/09/85.
10 Eps. 51 pages.
Script: Alan Grant.
Art: Carlos Ezquerra.
Reprinted: Best of 2000 AD Monthly 50.

Title: Max Bubba.
Progs 445-465.
From 23/11/85 to 12/04/85.
21 Eps. 107 pages.
Script: Alan Grant.
Art: Carlos Ezquerra.

Title: Smiley's World.
Progs 466-467.
From 19/04/86 to 26/04/86.
2 Eps. 9 pages.
Script: Alan Grant.
Art: Carlos Ezquerra.

Title: Rage.
Progs 469-489.
From 10/05/86 to 27/09/86.
21 Eps. 107 pages.
Script: Alan Grant.
Art: Carlos Ezquerra.

Title: Incident on Mayjer Minor.
Progs 490-496.
From 04/10/86 to 15/11/86.
7 Eps. 36 pages.
Script: Alan Grant.
Art: Carlos Ezquerra.

Title: Warzone!
Progs 497-499.
From 22/11/86 to 06/12/86.
3 Eps. 14 pages.
Script: Wagner/Grant.
Art: Carlos Ezquerra.

Title: Bitch.
Progs 505-529.
From 17/01/87 to 04/07/87.
25 Eps. 128 pages.
Script: Alan Grant.
Art: Carlos Ezquerra.

Title: Royal Affair, The.
Progs 532-536.
From 25/07/87 to 22/08/87.
5 Eps. 24 pages.
Script: Alan Grant.
Art: Carlos Ezquerra.

Title: Sorry Case, A.
Progs 540-543.
From 19/09/87 to 10/10/87.
4 Eps. 20 pages.
Script: Alan Grant.
Art: Colin MacNeil.

Title: Rammy, The.
Progs 544-553.
From 17/10/87 to 19/12/87.
10 Eps. 51 pages.
Script: Alan Grant.
Art: Carlos Ezquerra.

Title: Stone Killers, The.
Progs 560-572.
From 06/02/88 to 30/04/88.
13 Eps. 69 pages.
Script: Alan Grant.
Art: Carlos Ezquerra.

Title: Incident on Zeta.
Progs 573-573.
From 07/05/88 to.
1 Eps. 6 pages.
Script: Ezquerra/Grant.
Art: Carlos Ezquerra.

Title: No-Go Job, The.
Progs 580-587.
From 25/06/88 to 13/08/88.
8 Eps. 42 pages.
Script: Alan Grant.
Art: Simon Harrison.

Title: Final Solution, The.
Progs 600-647.
From 12/11/88 to 07/10/89.
23 Eps. 122 pages.
Script: Alan Grant.
Art: Simon Harrison.

Tyranny Rex

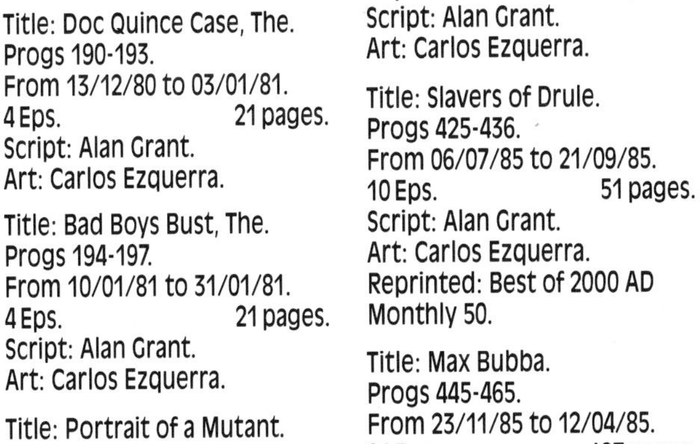

Universal Soldier

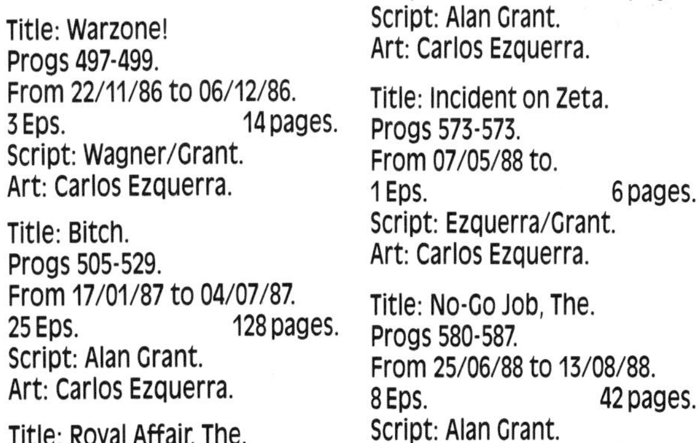

The VCs

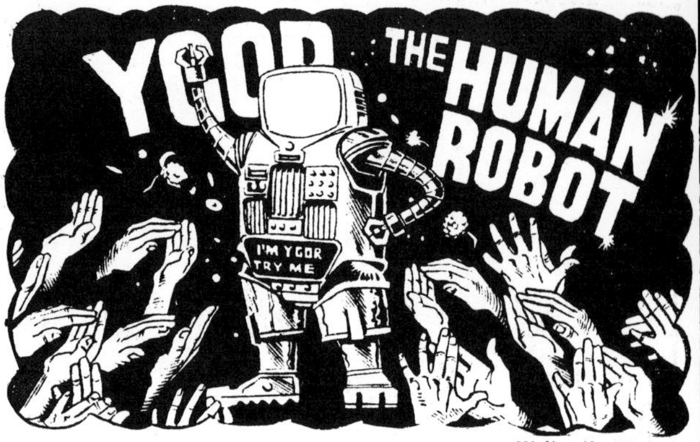

Walter the Wobot

Timequake

Title: Timequake.
Progs 148-151.
From 19/01/80 to 09/02/80.
4 Eps. 17 pages.
Script: Chris Lowder.
Art: Redondo.

Tribal Memories.

Title: Tribal Memories.
Progs 585-588.
From 30/07/88 to 20/08/88.
4 Eps. 20 pages.
Script: Pete Milligan.
Art: Tony Wright.

Tyranny Rex

Title: Tyranny Rex.
Progs 566-568.
From 19/03/88 to 02/04/88.
3 Eps. 15 pages.
Script: John Smith.
Art: Steve Dillon.

Title: Under Foreign Skies.
Progs 582-584.
From 09/07/88 to 23/07/88.
3 Eps. 15 pages.
Script: John Smith.
Art: Steve Dillon.

Title: Soft Bodies.
Progs 595-604.
From 08/10/88 to 10/12/88.
5 Eps. 28 pages.
Script: John Smith.
Art: Will Simpson.

Universal Soldier

Title: Universal Soldier.
Progs 537-543.
From 29/08/87 to 10/10/87.
6 Eps. 30 pages.
Script: Alan McKenzie.
Art: Will Simpson.

VCs, The

Title: VCs, The.
Progs 140-175.
From 24/11/79 to 30/08/80.
32 Eps. 129 pages.
Script: Gerry Finlay-Day.
Art: McMahon/Kennedy/Leach /Richardson.
Reprinted: Best of 2000 AD Monthly 31-33.

Visible Man, The

Title: Visible Man, The.
Progs 47-52.
From 14/01/78 to 18/02/78.
6 Eps. 29 pages.
Script: Pat Mills.
Art: Trigo/Montero.

Walter the Wobot

Title: Walter the Wobot.
Progs 50-68.
From 04/02/78 to 10/06/78.
13 Eps. 13 pages.
Script: Joe Collins.
Art: Gibson/Bolland.

Title: Walter the Wobot Book 2.
Progs 84-85.
From 30/09/78 to 07/10/78.
2 Eps. 2 pages.
Script: G.P. Rice.
Art: Brendan McCarthy.

Zenith

Title: Zenith Phase 1.
Progs 535-550.
From 15/08/87 to 28/11/87.
16 Eps. 81 pages.
Script: Grant Morrison.
Art: Steve Yeowell.

Title: Maximan.
Progs 558-559.
From 23/01/88 to 30/01/88.
2 Eps. 10 pages.
Script: Grant Morrison.
Art: Steve Yeowell.

Title: Zenith Phase 2.
Progs 589-606.
From 27/08/88 to 24/12/88.
18 Eps. 92 pages.
Script: Grant Morrison.
Art: Steve Yeowell.

Title: Zenith Phase 3/Part 1.
Progs 626-634.
From 13/05/89 to 08/07/89.
9 Eps. 45 pages.
Script: Grant Morrison.
Art: Steve Yeowell.

Zippy Couriers

Title: Zippy Couriers.
Progs 610-611.
From 21/01/89 to 28/01/89.
2 Eps. 12 pages.
Script: Hilary Robinson.
Art: Graham Higgins.

Title: Butch.
Progs 613.
From 11/02/89.
1 Eps. 5 pages.
Script: Hilary Robinson.
Art: Graham Higgins.

Title: Supermarket.
Progs 618.
From 18/03/89.
1 Eps. 5 pages.
Script: Hilary Robinson.
Art: Graham Higgins.

Title: Women's Business.
Progs 622.
From 15/04/89.
1 Eps. 5 pages.
Script: Hilary Robinson.
Art: Graham Higgins.

Title: Searchers, The.
Progs 641-642.
From 26/08/89 to 02/09/89.
2 Eps. 10 pages.
Script: Hilary Robinson.
Art: Graham Higgins.

Zenith

Zippy Couriers

NU EARTH, THE MOROKK DESERT COMBAT ZONE. IN A SURPRISE NIGHT MOVE, A NORT COLUMN SWINGS SOUTH FOR THE CITY OF KYRO. . .
LAST SOUTHER EARLY-WARNING-SYSTEM SILENCED, SIR! THE ROAD TO KYRO'S CLEAR, BUT OUR AIR'S ALMOST USED UP!
DON'T WORRY—
ALL THE AIR WE WANT IS WAITING IN THE GASBAH. ONCE REPLENISHED, WE'LL TAKE KYRO—THEN THE ENTIRE ZONE!
KYRO
ROGUE TROOPER
THE GASBAH—Part 5
IN THE GASBAH, THE ALIEN QUARTER OF KYRO, NORT SECRET AGENTS HAD BEEN HARD AT WORK. . .
MILLIONS OF OXBOTTLES READY!
AND ANY INQUISITIVE FREAKS SILENCED, INCLUDING THE G.I. UPSTAIRS.
ROGUE HAD BEEN DRUGGED WITH A PARALYSING AGENT. . .
YEAH, NORTY—I'M FLAT ON MY BACK, BUT I'VE GOT A NEAT TRICK UP MY SLEEVE. . .

A 'BURSTER -BOMB. I'M GONNA BLOW THIS WHOLE DUMP OUT.
BUT FIRST I GOTTA GIVE THOSE ALIS OUT IN THE GASBAH A CHANCE TO GET CLEAR — BY USING BAGMAN'S SYNTH.
XX-OOO X AGGHA VE TSHO! <LISTEN ALL ALIENS — EVACUATE THE GASBAH NOW! SCATTER INTO KYRO, AND WARN THE HUMES!>
AHGGGHH?
THAT DAMN G.I., HE'S UP TO SOMETHING!
AHSSHHH!
GHHHHAA!
THE ALIENS ARE RUNNING!
I GAVE 'EM THEIR CHANCE... NOW TO MAKE A LITTLE NOISE BY THROWING THIS INTO THE CELLAR. I'LL TAKE MY CHANCES OF SURVIVING THE BLAST.
NO!
DAMN YOU, ROGUE, AND YOUR FAIR PLAY. YOU FOULED IT UP!
OUR AGENTS OUTSIDE ALERTED US, G.I....
TRY AND SURVIVE THIS!

RRIIIIIPPP!
AAAH!
SLASSH!
NO! MY PROTECTIVE SEAL!
SOME ALIS CAME BACK! THE 'BRUTALS' I MET ON MY FIRST EVENING HERE!
BAGMAN TRANSLATED FOR ROGUE. . .
<NOBODY TELLS US TO RUN WITHOUT KNOWING THE REASON WHY, G.I. YOU WANTED TO SAVE OUR LIVES, NOW WE'VE RETURNED THE COMPLIMENT.
THOSE TWO WON'T CAUSE YOU ANY MORE TROUBLE.>
<AND I CAN CARRY OUT YOUR PLAN. REMEMBER ME?>
THE HOTEL GUEST... FROM ROOMS SIX, SEVEN AND EIGHT!
MEANWHILE, ALIENS WERE STREAMING OUT OF ALL THE GASBAH EXITS. . .
WE CAN'T STOP THEM!
WHO CARES? OUR FORCES WILL SOON CONTROL ALL KYRO!
THE REST OF THE CITY HAD A HUMAN POPULATION —
ALIS OUT OF BOUNDS!
HOW DARE THEY COME INTO OUR DISTRICTS!
WAIT — THEY'RE TRYING TO TELL US SOMETHING!
XX-GS-AA!
ZAAL DE BOOP!
HE'S POINTING TO THE GASBAH! SOUNDS AS THOUGH SOMETHING BIG IS HAPPENING THERE! BETTER TAKE COVER!

MEANWHILE, IN THE DESERT...
BEING HAULED OUTTA THE CITY. THAT ALI'S GONNA GIVE HIS RIGHT 'ARM' TO STOP THE NORTS...
NO PROBLEM.
I CAN ALWAYS...
GROW...
ANOTHER!
STAK! 'BURSTER BOMB!
FSSSSSSSSS
KAABOOOM
GRIEF! DON'T KNOW WHAT CAUSED THAT, BUT. THANK GOD THE ALIS WARNED US!

IT APPEARS YOU SAVED OUR CITY, ER, FRIEND!
HEY—LOOK AT THE GASBAH!
THE BLOWOUT DISPERSED THE CHEM-CLOUDS! THE GASBAH AIN'T THE GASBAH ANY MORE!
IT'S BEEN CLEANED UP— IT'S BETTER THAN ANY OTHER QUARTER NOW!
ER, WE RECKON WE OUGHTA OFFER YOU THE FREEDOM OF THE CITY. IN OTHER WORDS— GET THE SAME RIGHTS AS US. WE OWE YOU THAT.
AHXHHAGA AIGHA!
SORRY, DON'T KNOW THE ALI LINGO YET, BUT WE'LL BE SURE TO LEARN.
MEANWHILE. . .
PARA-AGENT'S WEARING OFF, AND I'M GETTING MY STRENGTH BACK. THANKS, GUYS. IF MY RECKONING IS CORRECT, YOU'LL BE TREATED AS EQUALS NOW, BY THE CITIZENS OF KYRO.
IN KYRO THERE WAS CAUSE FOR MORE CELEBRATION. . .
JUST HEARD THEY'RE PICKING UP A NORT INFILTRATION COLUMN OUT IN THE DESERT. THE ZONE'S SECURE— SO DRINK ON IT!
X-XXXHA-HHAAAA.
THAT DUSK. . .
COLUMNS OF CAPTIVE NORTS, AND I'VE LIFTED THE BARRIERS ON THE GASBAH. 'CEPT, AS ALWAYS, I'M THE ONE LEFT ALIENATED IN THIS WAR.
FOR ONCE YOU FEEL A WHOLE LOT CLEANER.
C'MON, ROGUE— WALK THE LAND.
The End
2000 A.D. Credit Card:
SCRIPT ROBOT GERRY FINLEY-DAY
ART ROBOT CAM KENNEDY
LETTERING ROBOT BILL NUTTALL
COMPU·73E

Published by Fleetway Publications, Greater London House, Hampstead Rd, London NW1 7QQ, a member of Maxwell Consumer Publishing and Communications Ltd. Sole Agents: Australia and New Zealand, Gordon & Gotch Ltd, South Africa, Central News Agency Ltd. Printed in the UK by BPCC Paulton Books Ltd. Origination by Hoistmuir, Birmingham.

Strontium Dog
INCIDENT AT THE END OF THE WORLD
SO THIS IS THE WAY THE WORLD ENDS.
WITH THE SUN A GIANT DISC, REACHING OUT FLAMING TENDRILS TO STRANGLE ITS FAVOURITE CHILD.
WITH THE WATER GONE, AND THE SOIL BAKED TO CLAY, AND THE EARTH SPEWING UP HER MOLTEN GUTS.
WITH ALL OUR HOPES, AND DREAMS, AND SUFFERINGS JUST SO MUCH DUST BLOWING IN AN ACRID WIND.
NO MORE MUTANTS — NO MORE NORMS — NO MORE LIFE — AND SOON, NO MORE PLANET EARTH.
2000 AD
SCRIPT ALAN GRANT
ART KEITH PAGE
LETTERING KID ROBSON

DOC VELISOVSKY! I KNOW YOU'RE HERE!
MAKE IT EASY ON THE BOTH OF US— GIVE YOURSELF UP!
YOU HEAR ME, DOC? SURRENDER, AN' YOU CAN WALK OUT OF THIS ALIVE!
SUIT YOURSELF, DOC. I'LL JUST HAVE TO COME GET YOU!
STRANGE. LOOKS LIKE HE PICKED UP COMPANY.
WHAT KINDA BEAST LEFT A TRACK LIKE THAT?
I DON'T LIKE THIS. TIME CONTROL SAID IT WAS SO FAR IN THE FUTURE, ALL LIFE OUGHTA BE DEAD.
WON'T HURT TO TAKE A LOOK...

ALPHA RAYS STREAM FROM THE MUTANT BOUNTYHUNTER'S EYES, PIERCING THE ROCK AS IF IT WAS GLASS --
PSSSTTT!
OKAY, GUYS. DROP THE WEAPONS AN' RAISE THE HANDS!
YOUR FUNERAL, PAL!
DAMN! GUN'S NOT--
WAK
AAAH!

INONISED RADIATION MUST HAVE DAMAGED THE POWER PACK ! ONLY HOPE MY TIME GRENADES --
WEREN'T AFFECTED !
HURLED A MERE FRACTION OF A SECOND INTO THE PLANET'S PAST, THE TROLLS REAPPEARED A MILE AWAY--
WHILE JOHNNY ALPHA MOVED DEEPER INTO THE BOWELS OF A DYING PLANET--
WEIRD, MOVING DOWN THROUGH THE JUNK OF A MILLION YEARS, EACH NEW CIVILISATION BUILT ON THE RUINS OF THE LAST.
AND FOR WHAT ? TO ALL FINALLY COME TO NOTHING ON A WORLD THAT'S DRYING UP AND BLOWING AWAY.

MILTON KEYNES... SOME DAY ALL CITIES WOULD BE LIKE THIS, THEY SAID. AND NOW THEY ARE.
WELCOM TO MILTON KEYNE EUROPE'S B MUTANT GH
YOU BRUTES! LET ME GO! WHAT ARE YOU DOING? WHAT DO YOU WANT WITH--
me?
I ONLY GOT ONE MORE GRENADE — AN' THAT'S FOR THE TRIP HOME! JUST GONNA HAVE TO HOPE THESE CREATURES DON'T CALL MY BLUFF..!
FREEZE, ALL OF--
WHAT THE HELL..?

ALPHA!
THANK GOD YOU'RE HERE!
LISTEN—I MADE A MISTAKE ESCAPING. I SHOULD HAVE STAYED TO STAND TRIAL. I—I DON'T LIKE IT HERE! I WANT YOU TO TAKE ME BACK!
I'M NOT SURPRISED. END OF THE WORLD'S NOT THE CHEERIEST OF PLACES!
WONDER WHAT YOUR NEW FRIENDS WOULD SAY, THOUGH?
THEY'RE PRIMITIVES—THROWBACKS! THEY—THEY MUST HAVE FOUND THIS STATUE, AND NOW I'VE SHOWN UP IN PERSON, THEY THINK I'M SOME SORT OF **DIVINE BEING!** THEY'RE **WORSHIPPING** ME!
PLEASE, ALPHA—I WAS **WRONG** TO COME HERE! I'LL CONFESS TO EVERY CHARGE THE DOGHOUSE IS BRINGING AGAINST ME! JUST TAKE ME BACK—**PLEASE!**
EASY TO SAY THAT NOW, DOC. BUT I BET AS SOON AS YOU HIT 2170, YOU HIRE SOME FATCAT NORM LAWYER TO WEASEL YOU OUT OF IT!
AND YOU KNOW THE COURTS—YOU COULD BE GUILTY AS SATAN HIMSELF, BUT AS LONG AS YOU'RE NORMAL, NO CHARGE WILL EVER STICK!
I CAME HERE TO KILL YOU, VELISOVSKY...
N-NO! PLEASE--!